James Payn

The burnt million

Vol. III.

James Payn

The burnt million

Vol. III.

ISBN/EAN: 9783743377202

Manufactured in Europe, USA, Canada, Australia, Japa

Cover: Foto ©ninafisch / pixelio.de

Manufactured and distributed by brebook publishing software (www.brebook.com)

James Payn

The burnt million

THE BURNT MILLION

VOL. III.

NEW NOVELS AT ALL LIBRARIES.

SYRLIN. By OUIDA. 3 vols.

THE BISHOPS' BIBLE. By D. CHRISTIE MURRAY and HENRY HERMAN. 3 vols.

WITHOUT LOVE OR LICENCE. By HAWLEY SMART. 3 vols.

A YANKEE AT THE COURT OF KING ARTHUR. By MARK TWAIN. 1 vol.

A LAST LOVE. By GEORGES OHNET. 1 vol.

A NOBLE WOMAN. By HENRY GREVILLE. 1 vol.

THE HOLY ROSE &c. By WALTER BESANT. 1 vol.

PAUL JONES'S ALIAS &c. By D. CHRISTIE MURRAY and HENRY HERMAN. 1 vol.

THE LAWTON GIRL. By HAROLD FREDERIC. 1 vol.

THE FIRM OF GIRDLESTONE. By A. CONAN DOYLE. 1 vol.

THE MAN FROM MANCHESTER. By DICK DONOVAN. 1 vol.

SENTENCED! By SOMERVILLE GIBNEY. 1 vol.

A WAIF OF THE PLAINS. By BRET HARTE. 1 vol.

London: CHATTO & WINDUS, Piccadilly. W.

THE BURNT MILLION

BY

JAMES PAYN

AUTHOR OF 'BY PROXY' ETC.

IN THREE VOLUMES
VOL. III.

London
CHATTO & WINDUS, PICCADILLY
1890

PRINTED BY
SPOTTISWOODE AND CO., NEW-STREET SQUARE
LONDON

CONTENTS

OF

THE THIRD VOLUME

CHAPTER		PAGE
XXXV.	At Lunch	1
XXXVI.	Richard's Story	14
XXXVII.	The Story Continued	29
XXXVIII.	A Change of Front	44
XXXIX.	Plain Speaking	58
XL.	The Naked Truth	72
XLI.	Richard to the Rescue	86
XLII.	The Brothers	101
XLIII.	Method in his Madness	113
XLIV.	Difficulties	129
XLV.	Edward's Queen	145
XLVI.	'She is my Wife'	159
XLVII.	On the Spot	176
XLVIII.	A Comforter	192
XLIX.	Mr. Roscoe's Congratulations	205
L.	His Last Throw	219
LI.	Philippa Speaks Out	232
LII.	The Burnt Million	248
LIII.	Peace at Last	262

THE BURNT MILLION

CHAPTER XXXV

AT LUNCH

ON arriving at the Hall, Mr. Roscoe at once took Walter to his quarters at the cottage; he made some excuse about wishing him to take choice of one of two bedrooms, but his real reason was to introduce him to Richard.

Since his brother had been fool enough (as he expressed it to himself) to fall over head and ears in love with the girl, he thought it dangerous that he should have his first meeting with her accepted swain in the young lady's presence; he had confidence in

Richard's word, but not in his self-command. He almost feared that he might exhibit some sort of antagonism to the young fellow even as it was. It was, however, a groundless apprehension. So far from showing dislike or embarrassment, Richard received the newly-arrived guest with an excess of friendliness.

'I am glad, indeed,' he said, 'to take the hand of your father's son; it is a pleasure to which I have long looked forward, but which I began to fear I was never again to experience.'

'You knew him well, I know,' returned Walter with reciprocal warmth.

'He was the dearest friend I ever had,' was the other's earnest reply, 'and the best.' He scanned the young fellow from head to feet with curious interest. 'I see a likeness in you, stronger than when last I saw you as a boy, and yet not a strong one. He might have been in youth what you are;

but I only knew him in his latter years. Not that he was an old man, far from it; nor had fatigue and privation—though he had endured them to the uttermost— weakened his great strength.'

'Yes, he was very strong; and also, as I have heard, a most extraordinary runner,' said Walter.

'Yes, yes,' answered the other hastily; then added, as if to himself, 'Great Heaven, this is horrible!' and sank into a chair with stony eyes and bloodless face.

'My brother is not very well just now,' observed Mr. Roscoe; 'the least emotion excites him strongly. I warned you of this, you know, Richard,' he continued in an earnest, almost menacing tone.

'No, no, it is not *that*,' answered Richard vehemently. 'It is something of which you know nothing, but which it behoves Walter Sinclair to know. Leave us alone together, Edward.' Then, as his brother shook his head and frowned, he added, 'It is about his father, and his ears alone must hear it.'

'Then you can speak with him another time,' said Edward decisively; 'it will utterly upset you to do so now. Besides there is the luncheon bell, and it would be bad manners to detain Mr. Sinclair from his hostess, just after he has arrived. You know what a stickler she is about such matters.'

Walter had already had an experience of it, and at once hastened to take Mr. Roscoe's view of the matter.

'Nothing will give me greater pleasure,' he said to Richard gently, 'than to speak with you about my father; but, as your brother says, perhaps it will be better to wait for a more favourable opportunity.'

Richard scarcely seemed to hear what the other was saying. 'He would talk of you by the hour,' he said, as if buried in reminiscence. "My poor lad that I shall never see again," he used to call you. And he never did—he never did.' The speaker's chin fell forward on his breast, and he said no more.

'Come,' said Mr. Roscoe, taking the young man by the arm, 'let us leave my brother alone for a little. He is doing himself harm by all this talk.' Then, as they walked away together, he told his companion how tender-hearted his brother was ('it runs in our family,' he said, ' but I have more self-restraint'); and how greatly attached he had been to Walter's father. 'Nevertheless, my brother only knew him (as he told you) in his later years, during which, as I hear, you had no communication with your father.'

'That is quite true,' sighed the young man; 'I never saw him, nor heard of him, after he started to hunt in the prairie, till I got tidings of his death. He was killed by the Indians.'

'So I understand,' said Mr. Roscoe, a

little dryly for a member of such a tender-hearted family. 'Yonder are the ladies waiting for us, and also for their luncheon. I have noticed that the fair sex do not mind how late their guests are for dinner, but are very particular about the midday meal. It is doubtless because they are always taking little sips and snacks in the afternoon, and have no real appetite for the other.'

To look at Mr. Roscoe's smiling face, however, as it met those of his hostesses, you would have imagined he had just been passing a eulogium upon all womankind. Nor were they backward in reciprocating his apparent chivalry. Agnes dowered him with an especially gracious look, as if anxious to make amends for her late outbreak; Philippa smiled on him with satisfaction, at the remembrance of that passage of arms, which she well knew, moreover, that he had not forgotten; and Grace was radiant, though it was true not so much on his account as on that of the guest he had brought with him.

'Where is Mr. Richard?' inquired Agnes, as they sat down to table.

And before even Mr. Roscoe's ready tongue could frame an excuse for his brother's absence, Mr. Richard himself made his appearance. Every trace of his recent emotion had disappeared. *His* face, too, was pleasant and smiling; though to an observant eye (and there was one upon him) his cheerfulness might have seemed a little feigned.

'I am glad to see you looking so much better, Mr. Richard,' said Agnes; 'now our little family circle is quite complete.' She glanced at Mr. Roscoe for approval, for the word 'family' had been put in to please him; partly as a compliment to himself and his brother, partly to carry out his views as respected Grace and Walter.

'It will certainly not be the fault of our hostess,' that gentleman returned earnestly 'if it is not a happy one, and all does not go as merrily as a marriage bell.'

If a certain lawyer had been there, who was acquainted with the circumstances, he would probably have murmured to himself, 'What an infernal scoundrel!' but that individual was not present, and all who were seemed to receive the observation in a proper spirit. Curiously enough, however, the conversation presently reverted to him.

'Have you seen Mr. Allerton lately?' inquired Philippa of Walter.

'Yes; I saw him just before my departure from town, and he charged me with many kind messages to you ladies, which, except as to their general purport, I am very much afraid I have forgotten.'

'You had something else to think about, I dare say,' said Agnes, with another conciliatory glance at Mr. Roscoe.

'Or perhaps it was jealousy,' observed Philippa, with a sly look at Grace; 'some people don't like to give tender messages to ladies which have been entrusted to them by others. Not that I feel the omission very poignantly on my own account,' she added, 'for my experience of Mr. Allerton is far from tender. In his character of trustee I find him very hard.' Here she suddenly flushed up, and came to a full stop. Mr. Roscoe had (I grieve to say it of one generally so polite to ladies) given her a kick under the table.

'I cannot say that of him,' remarked Agnes coldly. 'He always seems to me to exercise a very proper prudence.'

Mr. Roscoe's face grew livid; Agnes, perhaps purposely, was looking elsewhere, and did not perceive it. 'You are a great friend of Mr. Allerton's, I believe, Mr. Sinclair,' she continued.

'He has been very kind to me at all events,' responded the young man warmly. 'Indeed I owe him a great deal, for, thanks to his good offices, when my Cumberland holiday is over, a position has been offered me in a certain firm, better than one so inexperienced as myself could have hoped for.

'That is very good news,' observed Mr. Roscoe, and he spoke as if he meant it, as indeed he did, for the tidings suited well with his own plans.

'But at present, Mr. Sinclair,' put in Agnes graciously, 'you will have nothing to do, I trust, but to enjoy yourself.'

She really liked the young fellow, but was also very desirous to efface from his mind the impression which her conduct of the morning had only too probably made upon it.

'Indeed, Miss Tremenhere, with the recollection of your late river home in my mind,' he answered gratefully, 'I can imagine nothing but happiness under your roof.'

Walter meant what he said, but his words to those present, and who knew how life went on at Halswater, must have seemed, indeed, a strange stretch of fancy. There was a sudden silence, which he naturally attributed to another cause. 'I do not forget, however,' he continued with feeling, 'that at Elm Place you had a guest whom we shall all miss here.'

'Yes, poor Lord Cheribert,' said Agnes, 'how affable he was, was he not?' She was not generally so maladroit in her observations, but she was in a hurry to say something.

'So full of high spirits, I should rather call him,' observed Philippa decisively. 'One never remembered that he was a lord at all.'

This was not quite true, as regarded herself; for indeed she had never forgotten the fact, which gave her an unreasonable pleasure, for a single instant; but to 'wipe her sister's eye,' as Mr. Roscoe called it, was a temptation she could never resist. Agnes bit her lip, angry with herself at her mistake, and furious with her reprover.

Unhappily, though he did not intend it, Mr. Roscoe's next observation followed Philippa's lead.

'Yes; one forgot his rank,' he said, 'in his attractive qualities; one called him "Cheribert" from the first; he was a capital fellow all round; it was a pity, however, that his great fortune went to the dogs, or rather to the horses.'

'Other people waste their money quite as foolishly,' observed Agnes dryly, 'though not on the same follies.'

Again came that livid look on Mr. Roscoe's face which had overspread it by the lakeside that morning. If ever an angry woman could be warned, it should have had a warning in it.

'For my part,' said Grace, speaking for the first time, and with suppressed feeling, 'I shall never think of Lord Cheribert's follies. He had many and great temptations to which others are not exposed. His faults were on the surface; few kinder, nay, even nobler hearts than his ever beat in a human breast.'

'In that I must entirely agree with you,' said Walter earnestly; 'and if he had lived he would have proved it.'

CHAPTER XXXVI

RICHARD'S STORY

THERE was something—'there is always a something'—on Grace's mind, beside the happiness which well-nigh filled it, in the consciousness that it behoved her to write to Mr. Allerton to tell him of her engagement.

Her correspondence with him had been hitherto always of a pleasant kind, but she foresaw that what she had now to say would be far from pleasing to him. She liked the old lawyer very much—more perhaps than any one in the world with one exception—but she knew his weakness. He was liberal even to munificence with his own money; quite understood that the only true value of it lay in its power of doing good; but he set too great store upon it when it belonged to other people. Half his life had been passed in the endeavour to make men come by their own, 'or to prevent what was theirs falling into other hands. Money was a sacred trust with him. If she had understood Mr. Allerton's real opinion of her sisters, and especially of Mr. Roscoe, she would have pictured to herself a far more vehement opposition; but even as it was, she knew that he would oppose her views. She did not fear that he would offer any personal objection—indeed how *could* he, or for that matter how could any one else?—but she felt that he would object to the pecuniary loss she would sustain by becoming Walter's wife. She had told Walter that the gulf between them was neither so wide nor so deep as he had imagined; and he had understood her as she knew (and meant him so to understand it) in the literal sense of her words. She had in reality referred to her indifference to the disparity of fortune between them; what he had imagined her to convey was that that disparity was not so very great; he was probably unaware that through her marriage with him she would forfeit her claim to an immense fortune; that nothing in fact would remain to her but the money she had saved since her father's death—much of which had gone in charity—and the 10,000*l*. he had left to her, let her marry whom she might. To what is called a chivalrous mind—but she knew it was not true chivalry; to a quixotic mind then, such as she feared that of Walter to be, the knowledge of all this might be fatal to his hopes. She felt that the longer it was delayed the better: that every day they passed in each other's society would make him more and more her own, and render it more difficult for him to give her up. The wisdom of the serpent and the harmlessness of the dove (or the love bird) combined to prevent her communicating at present with Mr. Allerton;

and she therefore forbore to do it. She had no fear of any one else telling him her secret. She was not so simple but that she perceived her sisters were very willing for their own sakes that she should marry Walter, and would certainly do nothing to obstruct it; and she blessed them for their greed.

In the meantime she had never been so happy.

> Love took up the glass of Time and turned it in his glowing hands;
> Every moment, lightly shaken, ran itself in golden sands.

If dear papa could have only known her Walter and witnessed her happiness, was the only picture her imagination could form of an increase of bliss.

> Many an evening by the waters (where, thank Heaven, were no ships)
> Did their spirits meet together at the touching of the lips.

The loneliness of Halswater made it an admirable locality for such proceedings, and Walter Sinclair was no laggard in love: never was an engaged young couple more completely left to their own devices than they were. Walter was a *persona grata* to every one, even including Richard Roscoe. They might have noticed indeed (but they noticed nothing) that he avoided them when together, with even a greater consideration than did the rest of the household, and that he shrank still more from meeting Grace alone; but he not only cultivated Walter's society, but showed a particular kindness for the young fellow.

It was many days, however, before he made that revelation he had promised him on their first acquaintance, respecting his connection with his father.

The three men had been smoking together at the cottage one night as their custom was after they had bidden good-night to the ladies, and Edward Roscoe, feeling tired, had gone to his own room. There had ensued a long silence between the two who remained, Walter's thoughts, as usual, being occupied with Grace, while the other, as he slowly. expelled the smoke from his lips, regarded his companion with earnest eyes and an expression which it would have been difficult to analyse, for it was made up of various emotions, and some of them antagonistic to one another—tenderness, remorse, and jealousy.

'Walter, my lad,' he presently said, in low grave tones, 'I hope we shall always be good friends whatever happens.'

'I hope so, indeed, Mr. Richard,' replied the young fellow, with a natural surprise. 'On my side at least it must always be so; not only on your own account but because you were my father's friend. I trust there is no reason why you should look forward, on your part, to any alteration in your feelings towards myself.'

'There will be no alteration, no,' answered the other with a heavy sigh. 'You will never do any harm to *me* more than you have already done.'

'And that is none,' returned Walter, with a light laugh, 'so I think our friendship is secure.'

He had not the least idea to what the other alluded; but his strange remark had made little impression upon him; he was not easily impressed just now by observations made by any one, save one, and Richard had always seemed to him a queer fellow, who lived more in the past than the present, and who had a way of speaking not always quite to the purpose.

'Heaven grant that it may be so,' continued his companion with gentle earnestness, 'but you, at all events, have something to forgive *me*, my lad; for but for Richard Roscoe, your poor father would have been alive this moment.'

'What? Did you kill him then?' cried Walter, starting from his seat.

'*I* kill him? *I* who was his dearest friend! No; though in one sense would that I had. From my hand he would have welcomed death rather than—' He broke off with a shudder, and the whispered words, 'Ah, how can Heaven permit such things?'

Walter resumed his seat, and waited with patient anxiety for what might be coming. It was obviously useless to press his companion; the difficulty he found in making his communication at all was only too evident. His face was grey and bloodless, and a dew, as of death itself, had fallen on it.

'There are people, Walter,' he commenced slowly after a long pause, 'who will tell you that the American Indians are as other men, with the like feelings and emotions as ourselves, open to gratitude and moved by tenderness, and who can be influenced for good. I have lived among them for years, and can only say that I have never seen such a one. Within my experience, they have been all alike, treacherous, base, and heartless, and whenever the opportunity is offered of proving themselves so, incarnate fiends. They have many evil passions (as Heaven knows have we too), but one overmastering one, that of cruelty; a lust for barbarity more hellish than ever dwelt in a white man's breast. This they have not in war time only but at all times, and directed not necessarily against their enemies but against all the human race. Your father understood this thoroughly; before he became a hunter, you know, he was attached as a volunteer to a detachment of the United States army; and this, he told me, happened to a little drummer boy of his regiment who chanced to fall into the hands of the Apache Indians. He was but thirteen years old and a pretty boy, and he was given over to the tender mercies of the squaws. Everywhere else in the world almost such a captive would have excited pity in the breasts of women. *These* creatures did this: they stripped the child, tied him to a tree, and for four hours subjected him to every torture which their experience told them would not be fatal to him. Then they took pine knobs, and, splitting them in small splinters, stuck them all over his little body, till (as a spectator, a Mexican half-breed described it) he looked like a porcupine, and set fire to them. They yelled and danced at his screams of anguish till he slowly died.'

'What a sickening tale!' exclaimed Walter, with marked disgust.

'No doubt,' replied the other dryly, 'but if such things are so bad even to hear of, what must they be to endure? If Indians so use a harmless child, you may guess what they are capable of when their enemies are in their power; I say their enemies—though they treat helpless women even more devilishly than they treat men. However, it was an enemy of theirs with whom my story has to do.'

'Did my father fall into the power of such fiends?' exclaimed Walter excitedly.

'Listen. Your father and I were hunters of the plains for years together. He was a man of iron nerve and an excellent shot, but, so far as I know, he never took a human life unless his own was threatened. Many and many a time had we been attacked by these devils, and sent them howling to their hell; but we never sought them out, nor even pursued them. He was a quiet man, neither given to bloodthirstiness nor revenge. So was I at that time, Heaven knows. It is not so now.' Then he paused and poured himself out a glass of water; his hand trembled so violently that he could hardly carry it to his lips. 'I cannot speak of these things as I would wish to do,' he murmured apologetically; 'there is a fever in my heart, and in my brain. They make me mad. Yes; he spared many that he might have slain, though he well understood their natures. We were well armed of course; one night as we were putting by our revolvers, I noticed he had a pistol in his breast-pocket. "What is that for?" I asked. "It is for myself," he answered gravely; "if the worst should come to the worst, I will never fall into Indian hands alive. I know them," he added significantly.

'We had had a good season and were returning to the settlement; we had left the prairie behind us when it became necessary one evening to cross a river. It was in flood and dangerous, but the Sioux were about us, we knew, and there was better and safer camping ground on the other side of it. We rode our horses at the stream, but it proved too strong for us. There were rocks too in the river, and against one of these I was dashed by the current and unhorsed. The animal was carried down the stream, and I myself reached the bank with difficulty; I was much bruised and had sprained my ankle.

Your father with great exertion brought his horse safe to land, but, like myself, at the sacrifice of his weapons; our rifles and revolvers were lost; he had nothing but his pistol. Our situation was desperate indeed, for we felt only too certain that we had been watched by the Sioux. Had we had our arms, we should not have feared them, for they had had experience of their accuracy, and relied on opportunity alone for destroying us. Worthless though they be, these wretches never throw their own lives away. If we had had even our horses we could have escaped from them; but we had but one horse. *That* they knew, but not that we were defenceless, so that for the night we were left in peace, but not to rest. I sometimes think if we could have got rest that night, two lives might have been saved instead of one. The fatigue exhausted our strength. At the dawn of day we saw the Sioux; they had crossed the river, doubtless at some ford, and were coming towards us—some fifty mounted men. One held out a branch of a tree in token of amity. Your father smiled a bitter smile as he saw it. "They must think us in straits indeed," he said, " to suppose us willing to trust to their good faith." Then, turning to me, " There is not a moment to be lost, Richard. You are lame and cannot run a yard. You must take my horse and ride for Railton (the nearest fort)."

'" What, and leave you to the tender mercies of these hell-hounds?" I answered.

'" Not so," he said, "I have my pistol, remember; it is but death at the worst. Moreover, by taking to the scrub yonder, I hope to keep ahead of them all, and save my scalp. You, of course, must keep to the open. My horse is a better one than was ever crossed by a Sioux. If you reach home with a whole skin, you will come back and look for me."

'" But you are throwing away your life for mine?" I cried.

'" Mount and ride, man. Every moment of delay is risking both our lives." He helped me on to his horse—for I was so stiff as well as lame that I could hardly move—with his own hands, and off we started, he for the scrub and I for the open. That was the last I saw of your father—alive.'

CHAPTER XXXVII

THE STORY CONTINUED

'WHY do you not go on?' inquired Walter, after a long silence, which his companion showed no disposition to break.

'There is a reason for it,' answered the other hoarsely; 'it would spare both of us if I said no more. Nevertheless, you have a right to hear all—if you wish it.'

Walter inclined his head; he felt too sick at heart to speak.

'Well, the good horse saved me from the Sioux, as he would have saved his master. They followed me for two days and then gave up the chase. On the third morning I reached the post, half dead with hunger and fatigue; but in an hour I was in the saddle again following my own tracks with five-and-twenty mounted volunteers. The fever of my soul sustained me. The thought of your father and of what he had done for me, and of what might have happened to him, filled my veins with fire. I slept at times upon my horse, but the men who were with me never lost the trail. Since your father had been bound for the same post, and we did not meet with him, I felt only too sure that he had not escaped with life. The best that we could look for, as I was well convinced, was to find his dead body, with a pistol bullet in it. But, alas, that was not to be. We searched as well as we could, always, however, moving quickly, till we came upon the scrub which I had seen him enter. To look for him there would have taken too much time, and it would be easy to return to it. The Indians had retired across the river; we found the ford and followed them.' Here Richard Roscoe paused and wiped his face, on which a ghastly dew was gathering. 'Shall I go on?' he murmured.

'Go on,' answered Walter, in tones that no one who knew him would have recognised for his own; his voice was frozen with the horror that had seized his companion, though he was ignorant of what was to come.

'Three miles or so from the river, we found what had once been a man, and your father. His head alone was above the earth, the rest of him they had buried standing. His poor limbs were bound with ropes. They had scalped him; they had cut off his lips, his eyelids, his nose and ears, and had left him then—still alive as we afterwards discovered—to be driven mad by the hot sun beating on his head, and to be revived for fresh tortures, by the cool air of the morning; Hell only knows for how long.'

Walter groaned.

'A hunter who heard of it from the fiends themselves says " the warrior " who invented this torture was thought very highly of by the tribe. There were not many left before we had done with them to praise him. This hand, palsied as it looks, slew seven of them!'

'Let me take it,' cried Walter hoarsely. He took it and kissed it.

'Yet, but for me, your father might have been alive, lad; and I should have suffered in his stead. Do you indeed forgive me?'

'Yes; if you had been in his place you would have done as he did.'

'I hope so; I think so; but he *did* it. If I ever forget it, I shall deserve to fall into Indian hands. Do you wonder now why I hate Indians?'

'But the pistol?' groaned Walter, unable to entertain any abstract subject in the whirl and horror of his personal feelings. 'Why did he not shoot himself?'

'I suppose the powder had got wet when he crossed the river. What are you doing, lad?'

The young man had passed quickly into his own room, and through the open door could be seen placing things in his portmanteau—a revolver was the first of them.

'I am going away. I leave to-morrow for America!'

Richard rose, went into the other room, and laid his hand upon his arm.

'No,' he said, 'that way madness lies; look at me and do not doubt it.'

Walter looked up and beheld a face he did not know; pallid with hate, distorted with passion: a livid face—and also one in which, it was plain, reason had no longer a place.

'Do you suppose I have not done all that could be done,' shouted this apparition, and then laughed aloud. 'Seven with my own hand, and six times as many more by those of my men. There is not one of them alive: not one, not one. Will you make war against a race with your single arm? Leave that to me. You are not a madman as I am. Can't you see it? Come, come,' he continued, drawing his now unresisting companion back into the smoking-room, and speaking in less vehement tones. 'You must keep your wits for other things; for you may need them. No. There has been mischief enough already done. Your father's torments have not been unavenged; the man for whom he sacrificed his life has had his sufferings too—and because of him. Above all things never breathe one word to *her* about your father's death. Do you hear me?'

'Whom do you mean by *her*?'

'Why, Grace, of course; our Grace. It would distress her.'

'Of course I shall never tell her.'

'You think so now; but perhaps at some other time; in years to come. Swear to me you will never tell her how I took your father's horse and rode away from him, and left him to his doom. Swear it.'

'I swear I never will.'

'I am satisfied; you are your father's son, and he never lied to me. Now let us talk of something else.'

The speaker's face had suddenly changed; the fire had fled from it, and also the remorse and pain; he looked like one exhausted even to the verge of death, but who, after a paroxysm of excitement, had returned to his right mind. The spectacle in some sort relieved his companion from the distress which the other's recital had caused him; was it possible, he wondered for the moment, whether the man was not a madman, and had imagined the whole hideous story; though he came to the conclusion that this was not the case, but rather that the recollection of so shocking an incident had affected his brain. The idea turned his thoughts into another channel. If the poor fellow should be subject, as he had himself confessed, to lose his reason, might he not prove dangerous to Grace? She was evidently a subject of regard to his disordered mind. His solicitude that she should not hear the story might be accounted for by the part he had himself played in it, but what did he mean by that strange expression 'our Grace'? It was a slight matter, but the least suspicion of danger in connection with so dear a being, alarmed him. There had hitherto not been the slightest kink or hitch in the smooth course of their true love, and he was the more inclined on that account to exaggerate the smallest obstacle to it.

It was with great dissatisfaction, therefore, that he heard his companion presently return to the subject which he had himself spoken of as closed.

'It may be necessary, my lad,' said Richard, as if moved by an afterthought, 'to speak of your father to you once again; but I see how the matter distresses you, as well it may, and I promise you it shall be for the last time.'

'Indeed,' returned the other earnestly, 'I

do not wish to hear it. What has been told me is sufficient, and more than sufficient. You were quite right to tell it me, and I thank you for the confidence that has cost you so dearly; but since, as you have justly pointed out, retribution is out of my power to exact, I entreat you to be silent on the matter, which can only cause me more distress and pain.'

'Poor lad,' answered the other with gentle gravity; 'perhaps it may not be necessary for me to speak; let us hope it may not for both our sakes. It is very late; good night; and may you have no such dreams as I have.'

Walter had no dreams that night for he had no sleep. The fate of his father, and the possibility of danger to Grace—or at the best of great distress of mind if she should come to hear of what had been confided to him, divided his waking thoughts. It is true that Richard had himself enjoined upon him silence on the subject; but what trust could be reposed in one so strange and excitable? it was even possible that he might tell the story to her with his own lips by way of penance for what he considered (though such an imputation was itself a proof of a disordered mind) his base behaviour. On the whole he decided to warn her of Richard, but in a way that should not arouse any serious apprehensions. The next day, therefore, he took an opportunity, while walking with her alone, of asking her how she liked her guest at the cottage.

'I like the poor fellow very much,' she replied frankly, 'better, indeed, than his brother, though we have known him so much longer.'

'Then why, since he has won your regard, my dear,' he answered smiling, 'should he be called a poor fellow?'

'Well,' returned Grace, with a little hesitation, 'he is an invalid, you know. One cannot but pity one who, though so far from old age, has lost the activity and strength that he manifestly once possessed. As he once told me with his own lips, he is the mere wreck of his former self. You are not jealous, *are* you?' she added slyly, 'that Mr. Richard has given me his confidences?'

'Not at all,' said Walter with a laugh, which was, however, rather forced, for her reply had chimed in with his apprehensions; 'but is there no other reason why you pity him?'

'Well, if you compel me to say so, I fear that the fatigues and privations he has endured have affected his mind as well as his body.'

'But you don't fear him, I hope,' inquired Walter anxiously.

'Certainly not; I believe he has a sincere regard for me. But there is no doubt that his manner is at times exceedingly eccentric.'

'Yes; some subjects excite him in the

strangest manner; he is not himself when he talks about them, and all allusion to them should be discouraged. I want you to be careful, my darling, about that—for his sake, of course.'

'I will be very careful; but what are the subjects?'

'Well, there is one, for example, which if he attempt to speak to you upon, I beg that you will decline to listen to him. Would you mind saying at once and peremptorily that it is distasteful to you?'

'I am quite sure that if I even hinted at it being so, it would be dropped at once. Mr. Richard, despite some drawbacks patent to everybody, is at heart a gentleman, and moreover would, I am convinced, respect any wish of mine.'

'Very good, then don't let him talk to you about the American Indians.'

'The American Indians?' echoed Grace, with amazement.

'Yes; it seems ludicrous enough, of course, but he has, not without reason, a great detestation of them. He has doubtless suffered at their hands, but his views upon the subject are exaggerated, and between ourselves by no means trustworthy. You must never be frightened by anything he tells you about them, but what will be much your safest way is to refuse to listen to him. When he gets upon that topic he is in my opinion not a responsible being. I hope I have not alarmed you, my darling,' for Grace had turned rather pale; 'there is no danger to be apprehended, of course, but I wish to save you from hearing what may be unpleasant, and which at the same time would be harmful to the poor man himself.'

'I am not the least afraid, Walter,' she answered quietly, 'and will take care to use the precaution you have recommended.'

They went on to talk of other subjects, and Walter, no doubt, thought he had reason to congratulate himself on his skilful diplomacy. But his revelation had filled Grace's mind with recollections and suspicions of which he little guessed. She was under a promise to Richard, as we know, to be silent about his extraordinary behaviour during their drive in the pony carriage, but the cause of it was no longer inexplicable to her. The strange noise they had heard as they approached the circus was no doubt the war whoop of the Indians, which had probably awakened some dreadful reminiscence in Richard Roscoe's mind. She recalled his look of horror and, as she now understood it, of undying hate when it fell upon his ear. Another thing, too, occurred to her which moved her even more—the attempt which, if his story was to be believed, had been made upon the life of the Indian on the fells. Was it possible that Richard Roscoe was the person who had assaulted him? The man's account of the affair had been received with incredulity, from the total absence of motive for such a crime. But if what she had just heard was true, there *was* a motive, and one that could have actuated one individual only in that neighbourhood—namely, Richard himself. She could not look upon him as a murderer, even in intent; her whole soul shrank from it; but the only alternative was irresistible, and filled her with vague alarms. On one point, at least—and why not on others?—their guest at the cottage was a madman.

CHAPTER XXXVIII

A CHANGE OF FRONT

IN his various characters as friend of the family, confidential adviser, and major domo, at Halswater, Mr. Edward Roscoe exercised a great many rights and privileges which no one ever thought of disputing; and among them was the unimportant but delicate office of opening the letter-bag, of which he kept the key. The post, as has been mentioned, came somewhat late in the day, so that instead of the family correspondence arriving as usual at breakfast time, and being displayed in public, it was brought to Mr. Roscoe, generally alone in his private sitting-room at the time, and distributed subsequently with his own gracious hands. Heaven forbid we should hint that he took any undue advantage of the circumstance, but it naturally happened that he knew who got letters, and also who sent them away. He knew, for example, that Grace had not yet written to Mr. Allerton since Walter's arrival, and secretly applauded her for that maidenly reticence. He had much correspondence of his own, too, which it was highly undesirable should be laid upon the breakfast-table, and altogether the arrangement was a very convenient one.

On a certain morning, when the bag had been brought to him as usual, and, as usual, before unlocking it, he had locked his door, among its contents was a letter from America, addressed to his brother. 'So it's come at last, has it?' was his muttered observation, as he took the envelope in his hand and examined it attentively. 'What on earth made the fool seal it?'

The observation seemed uncalled for, for though it is now unusual to seal letters, to do so is not a proof of folly; and in some instances indeed the contrary. There was a little kettle on his fire—for he was a man who liked his coffee hot, and at irregular hours—and he now looked at it with an expression of great irritation. The fact was the kettle was useful to him in opening gummed envelopes, but of no use at all in opening sealed ones. Was it worth while to take the impression of this particular seal—which only bore initials on it—before breaking it or not? Considering it was only Richard's letter, a fellow who took no notice of such little matters, he thought it was not worth while; he would melt the wax, and after possessing himself of the contents of the epistle, fasten it down again with a blank seal. It was a simple operation, and one to which he was well accustomed; he melted the seal and opened the envelope. It contained a short official note to his brother, just saying, 'I forward you what you left with me,' with a banker's name attached and the enclosure.

This latter was in another envelope also sealed, directed 'To my dear son, Walter, to be delivered into his own hands.' 'Not just yet, however,' was Mr. Roscoe's grim remark, as he melted this second seal. Then he read the enclosure. The effect of its perusal was remarkable. What he said cannot be written, because it was an execration of extreme violence, 'both loud and deep,' but what he did was to stamp upon the ground with impotent rage. His countenance was white with the white heat of fury, and the consciousness of baffled schemes. His eyes flashed fire. His first impulse was to burn the letter, but even as he held it over the glowing coals, he hesitated, and at that moment he heard Miss Agnes's voice at the door of the cottage asking if the letters had come.

In an instant he had thrown it into his open desk, and locked the desk, and came out to her, smiling, with the opened bag in his hand.

'There are no letters for you, Miss Agnes, and I, too, have been neglected by my correspondents; but there is one for Miss Grace—I fancy from Mr. Allerton.'

The word 'fancy' was a pretty touch, for the lawyer's hand was as familiar to him as his own, and many a letter from him had he read, though he had never been one of his correspondents. If he had read this one, which he had had no time to do, it would have given him less dissatisfaction than some others, which, indeed, had spoken of Mr. Edward Roscoe with more freedom than friendship.

Agnes held him in honeyed talk, as was her wont when she got him alone; and to see his eyes and his smile as they replied to her, one would have thought the lady very dear to him, and never have guessed the impatience which her presence evoked, and far less the passion that was consuming him in which she had no part at all. At last he got rid of her and returned to his own room, a different man from him who had last entered it. An hour ago, though there was much to trouble him, and obstacles in his path that would have daunted a less determined spirit, the immediate matter which he had in hand had been going well and prosperously. It was only an initial difficulty in his far-reaching plans, it is true, but to find one impediment in course of removal had been a satisfaction to him; and lo! instead of its being swept away, it had assumed even greater proportions, and all the work he had had with it had now, under far less encouraging circumstances, to be done over again. In vain he pulled at his cigar, not for comfort (comfort even from the soothing weed was not for such as he), but for ideas—how to meet this unexpected blow, and especially how to turn it, as he had often done in the case of such disappointments, to his own profit. For nearly an hour he could find no way out of the maze of difficulty, and only confused himself in his efforts to find it; but at last he hit upon a plan. It was a dangerous, even a desperate one, and, what was worst of all, required the connivance and assistance of others; but, having once grasped it, his hold on it grew more tenacious with every moment of possession. It is a characteristic of men of his class, fertile in schemes, sanguine of success, and confident in their own powers of persuasion, that nothing but total and complete failure can make them doubt of the practicability of their plans. What is also an attribute of theirs is promptness; not an hour, not a minute, do they waste in putting them into execution. Taking the fateful scroll (or scrawl, for it was written in shaky and ill-formed characters, significant of a tumult of anxieties in the writer's mind) from the desk, he placed it carefully in his breast pocket, and sought the presence of the very person from whom he had of late so gladly parted, Agnes Tremenhere.

Each of the elder sisters had, like Grace, her own boudoir, and there was no sort of difficulty—for he had often certain business of a private character to transact with both of them—in seeing his hostess alone. She received him even more cordially than usual, for his business was not always of a welcome character, and as he had had no letters from town that day she justly concluded that it was not on business that he came. It was soon made plain, however, that he had not come on pleasure.

'Agnes,' he said, as soon as he had closed the door behind him, 'a great misfortune has happened to us—or so, at least, it at first seemed to me. Before telling you how I propose to meet it, and even turn it to our advantage, I wish you to be informed exactly of its nature. Read *this*,' and, without more words he placed the missive that had been sent to his brother in her unfaltering hand.

When not moved by jealousy or wrong,

Agnes Tremenhere was cold and calculating enough. Her disposition, indeed, though far gentler, was almost as practical as that of Mr. Roscoe himself, and of this he was well aware. He was convinced that of the various persons with whom he was compelled to deal upon the present occasion, Agnes would be the least difficult to manage, and the most likely to fall in with his views. Nevertheless, it was with satisfaction that, as he watched her face attentively as she read, he saw it harden, after the first flush of surprise, and assume an expression of unswerving determination.

'You know what this means, of course, as regards ourselves,' he said, 'and also Philippa' (this he added incidentally), 'if what we once thought so advisable should come to pass?'

'It would be the perpetration of an infamy,' she answered, in a voice hoarse with rage. 'It would be giving effect to a most wicked wrong.'

'No doubt; and therefore we must take measures to put a stop to it.'

'It will be very difficult, Edward, as well as cruel, now that matters have gone so far.'

There was a touch of softness in her tone, and though only a touch it alarmed him.

'Of course it will be difficult,' he answered, with grim contempt. 'As to the cruelty, that is all nonsense; I mean, of course' (for he saw a flush of indignation glow on his companion's face), 'that a girl like Grace is too young to know her own mind, and will not suffer as you and I would do under similar circumstances. For all that she has said, I still believe that she had a tenderness for Cheribert, and if this Sinclair was got rid of, she would find some other man equally to her mind. Let us confine ourselves to the difficulty. It is great, I admit, but not insuperable. The question I have come to ask you is whether you are prepared to see the vast fortune your father left behind him pass out of the family, or into one branch of it——'

'I am not,' she put in quickly. 'I will never submit to such a wrong if I can help it. There is nothing I would not do—provided, of course, that it were not itself a wrong—to prevent its commission.'

'That is spoken like yourself, Agnes,' said Mr. Roscoe, approvingly. 'I only hope I shall find others, to whom I must also look for assistance, as just and reasonable.'

'Others? Do you mean Philippa?' she answered with knitted brow.

'Well, you see, my dear, her interests are equally threatened by this document with your own. We must all put our shoulders to the wheel, and work together for once.'

'We shall hardly have Grace with us, however,' observed Agnes dryly. 'I am truly sorry to have to treat the dear girl in any way as an antagonist. But she ought to be able to see for herself, how unfair and infamous——'

'So she would,' put in Mr. Roscoe hastily; 'if her eyes were not blinded by her love for Walter she would be the first to see it; we shall be in fact only working in the same interests as herself—namely in those of Truth and Justice—if she were in a position to look at the matter from an unprejudiced standpoint. As it is, however, she must know nothing about this,' and he tapped the document with his finger.

'And Richard?'

'Well, of course, Richard must never know. Why should he? The thing has been lost in the post, and there is no duplicate.'

'Must it really be so? I hate deceit, Edward.'

'So do I; but I hate injustice more—to those I love,' he added tenderly.

'When you say that, Edward, you make me feel for our poor Grace more than ever,' said Agnes softly. 'Yet, as you say, there seems no other way out of it. How is it you propose to break off the match?'

'Leave that to me, my dear, just for the present; I wish to avoid distressing your tender heart more than is absolutely necessary. When I need your help I will tell you all. But in the meantime you must gradually— very gradually—cease your civilities to Mr. Sinclair. He is sharp enough in taking a hint, so be very careful not to give him an opportunity of asking you the reason of your change of manner. Indeed I am going to take him in hand myself, so that he will probably not think it necessary to put that question. You must drop him as gently as if he was made of glass, but never let Grace herself perceive that you are dropping him. Her too, poor dear, I shall have to deal with, using, however, arguments very different from those in his case. Many difficulties lie before me, as you may suppose, Agnes, but you shall see that they are not insuperable.'

'You are a wonder, Edward,' she exclaimed with admiration. 'It is your marvellous gift of persuasion that makes me sometimes doubt of you myself.'

'Great Heavens, do you mean that you think I would deceive *you*, Agnes?' he exclaimed with indignation. 'This is a poor return indeed for long and loving service.'

'I only said sometimes, Edward,' she replied affectionately; 'you must not be hasty with your Agnes, even though she is sometimes hasty with you.'

'It is not your haste, my dear, but your impatience that I object to,' he answered with a smile; 'the present obstacle, however, will not, as you doubtless fear, delay our happiness, if all goes well with my plan.'

'I am glad to hear it indeed, for I am sick of delays, Edward,' she answered, laying her jewelled hand upon his shoulder tenderly.

'And so am I, dear Agnes,' and to do him justice he looked sick.

CHAPTER XXXIX

PLAIN SPEAKING

MR. ROSCOE had certainly no reason to be dissatisfied with the result of his interview with the head of the house. Agnes had agreed with his views, confessed herself as willing to assist his plans, and had almost forborne to question him about them. She had been content to leave matters in his hands, without even asking him what he had meant by saying that he had hoped to turn this misfortune that had happened to them to their own advantage. He would have told her if she had pressed him, but it was a relief to his mind—already so heavily weighted—that she had not done so. He was not grateful to her, however, because he knew that she had something to gain by her forbearance, and was also desirous to make up to him for the insolence (as he termed it) of her recent behaviour. Philippa he foresaw would not be so easily won over. She had not so much to gain by pleasing him, and nothing to atone for. He would have to explain his scheme to her, and it would be much more distasteful to her than it would have seemed to her sister; she was more sentimental and soft-hearted, or, as he put it to himself with his usual frankness, in all things that concerned the feelings a greater fool. On the other hand, there were reasons why he could 'say things' to Philippa which he could not venture upon with her elder sister. He could be more masterful with her, if need were, and also, strange to say, more tender without compromising himself. Indeed his very first act on entering her boudoir was to put his arm round her waist and kiss her.

'Goodness gracious!' she exclaimed, 'what is the matter, Edward?'

It was such a strange remark to make upon such an occurrence, had it been an unprecedented one, that we must take it for granted it had happened before; indeed, it was not his caress at all, but the expression of his face, which was very grave and sad, which had evoked it.

'A letter, my dear Philippa, has come to my brother to-day, which brings very bad news to you and me, and will require all your philosophy to bear it. Instead of an obstacle to our happiness being, as we fondly thought, removed, it threatens us with ruin.'

'With *ruin*?'

'Yes; with nothing less. It is no use deceiving ourselves upon that point, nor will it help us to reproach me for follies, as you have called them, of which I have been guilty. I will own I have been a fool at once, and so save time, which has become indeed an object to us. It is no longer a question of patience with us, but of now or never. Read *that*.' And he put the document into her hand with a deep-drawn sigh.

She read it with a frightened face, and none of the fury her sister had shown.

'This is indeed most cruel and unexpected,' she said.

'Unexpected? Why, of course it is,' he answered with irritation; 'but as to cruel, you refer, I suppose, to the measures which it will be necessary to take with Grace; you can hardly imagine that I intend it to take effect as regards ourselves.'

'But how is it possible to avert it?'

'Well, for one thing this marriage of course must be broken off.'

'Grace's marriage? Break off dear Grace's marriage with Walter? Oh, Edward, you could surely never have the heart to do it!'

'I mean to try, at all events,' he answered curtly. 'You must be a born idiot, Philippa, if you do not see the absolute necessity of it. A girl of her age is not so grievously to be pitied because she has made a false start in her first love venture. Women don't break their hearts about men whom they have only known for a few months.'

'I will never consent to parting them,' cried Philippa, bursting into tears.

'What? You prefer beggary, do you? Fortunately for you, I have an equal interest with yourself in this matter, and beggary will not suit *me*.'

'But why should there be anything of the kind, Edward? I know dear Grace's noble nature, and am very sure that when she comes to hear of this—for I conclude Walter has not told her——'

'I conclude so too,' interrupted Mr. Roscoe with bitter scorn, 'for I have good reason to believe that Walter does not know it himself. You may also be assured that he never will know it.'

'You have opened his letter then?'

'Most certainly I have. If you should ever dare to dream of telling him so, I would throw it in the fire, and have you locked up for a mad woman for having imagined such a story. Scruples indeed! *You* to have scruples! Have you forgotten how your father died?'

'Oh, Heaven have pity upon me, since man has none!' cried the wretched woman, throwing herself into a chair and bursting into a torrent of tears.

'I am sorry to have been compelled to allude to so painful an incident,' observed Mr. Roscoe coldly, ' but I cannot stand hypocrisy. You strain at a gnat after having swallowed a camel, hump and all. I really must decline to listen to such folly. I came here for your advice and assistance——'

'*My* advice!' she interrupted bitterly. 'When did you ever ask for my advice, or take it when it was offered?'

'What I understand you to propose, madam, is that we should throw ourselves upon the generosity of Mr. Walter Sinclair *per* Grace, his wife, and accept whatever terms he may in his magnanimity offer us. For my part I absolutely refuse to accept his charity. It would be too humiliating, and also, I am very sure, too limited. If *that* be your advice, you are correct in supposing that I think it worthless. Let me confine myself then to asking your assistance. I can get on without it, and as to any opposition on your part it would be fruitless, and you would repent it to the last hour of your life, though it would not perhaps be a very long one. Lives have been cut short in domestic circles before now——'

'Oh, spare me, spare me!' groaned the unhappy woman.

'By all means. I wish not only to spare you but to benefit you all I can, if you will only be a reasonable being. Though your help is not indispensable, it would be very welcome, and would certainly be of service in breaking the blow which necessity compels me to inflict upon your sister. I regret it as much as yourself, but I have a plan in my head which in the end may not only turn this seeming misfortune to our advantage, but console Miss Grace for the loss of her lover.'

'Console her?' answered Philippa with amazement. 'What can ever console a girl for such a loss?'

'Another lover.'

The suggestion was offered in all good faith, and without the least touch of sarcasm, but had the speaker guessed its effect upon his hearer he would have given a good deal to have recalled its utterance. There are some subjects on which it is very dangerous for a man to confess his cynicism to one of the other sex. Philippa made no answer, which gratified her companion, since it bespoke submission to his will, but what he had said had fallen upon the little spark of respect for him that was still alive in her breast, and extinguished it for ever. Love still survived there, as it will do long after respect is dead; but it was not the love it had been. Passion had long fled from it, Trust had well-nigh vanished too, and even Hope itself was on the wing.

'Yes, Philippa,' he continued after a long pause, 'it is my intention that Grace shall marry my brother Richard.'

Numb and dulled as the poor woman's feelings had become under the weight of that inevitable will, his words still evoked a shrill note of astonishment.

'Richard!'

'Yes; you women plume yourselves on your sagacity in such matters, but I'll wager that the notion of Richard being in love with your sister has never entered into your mind. I have perceived it, however, for many a day; it is only with the utmost difficulty that he can conceal his passion for her.'

The tidings interested while it shocked her; no matter how cramped and crushed may be a woman's heart, there is one subject to which it never ceases to vibrate with sympathy.

'He has concealed it,' she observed. 'I am certain that Grace knows nothing of it.'

'Of course not—not a word, not a whisper, thanks to me; any hint of it would have been most inconvenient, perhaps even detrimental to our plans. I persuaded him that his suit would be the maddest folly. It will be much easier to persuade him of the contrary. And if—as will as surely happen as I am a living man—these second nuptials shall be accomplished, instead of her having a husband of whose nature we know little, and who might have given us trouble in a hundred ways, she will have one who in my hands will be as clay to the potter, and so out of this nettle Danger we shall pluck the flower Safety.'

'And Grace?'

'Well, Grace of course will be our difficulty, although the only one. I have a plan, however, which, sooner or later, will succeed even with Grace. We cannot of course expect that she will transfer her affections from one to the other so quickly as would be desirable. In love affairs a girl is never reasonable; but still I have reasons, I think, that will not only persuade her to give Walter up, but will at least clear the way for Richard. She is well inclined to him already in a sisterly way. You don't think much of that, and I don't wonder; I use the phrase of course in its common acceptation, and she is *not* his sister. We all know what comes of such Platonic attachments, when no nearer one can be got. A woman who has been "disappointed," as she calls it, will marry out of pique rather than not marry at all. She feels the need of "something to cling to," and one stick will serve her turn as well as another.'

He paused, but there was no reply.

'Do you hear me, madam? Are you favouring me with your attention?' he inquired passionately.

'Oh, yes, I hear you!' answered Philippa despairingly, 'and alas! I understand you very well.'

'Then also heed. The help that I require from you is simply this: to cease from expressing any of that morbid sympathy which you have lavished—as it now turns out, have wasted—upon this interesting young couple. Without being rude to Walter, be cold and discouraging to him. Let him understand, but without giving him a pretext for asking for an explanation, that something has caused you to change your views of his pretensions. If he does ask, refer him to me. The task I set you is an easy one enough.'

'It is not easy,' she answered in broken tones, 'but since needs must, I will perform it.'

'There's a good girl!' He patted her

cheek—it was as cold as marble—as if she had been a child. 'You are about to do what is very distasteful to you, I know, and as you believe solely for my sake; but it is for both our sakes. We shall be stronger—you and I —when this has come to pass, against the common enemy. Grace's husband—and therefore Grace—will be on our side. Again I say that this document, which now seems so harmful to us, will prove beneficial to our interests.'

'What are you going to do with it?' she inquired in a faint voice.

'Well, that is my business. I shall probably put it in the fire. Now I am going to Grace.'

'With that in your pocket?' she murmured apprehensively.

'Why not? She can no more read it through this cloth'—and he tapped his breast —'than she can read my heart on the other side of it. It will be the hardest morning's work that I have ever had to do; but " men must work and women must weep," is the sentence that Fate has passed upon us. Goodbye, my dear, and wish me well through with it,' and once more he touched her cheek with his false lips.

She forced a smile as he left her, but it vanished as the door closed behind him, and was succeeded by a look of misery and despair.

'Wish him well!'—no, she did not even wish herself well. It was blasphemy to hope that good would come to anybody from what he was about to do. She pitied Grace from the bottom of her soul, but she pitied herself too. If Grace were doomed to lose her lover, she too had lost faith in the man to whom she had given her love. '" She cannot read my heart," he said,' she moaned piteously; 'how should she when he has no heart to read?'

CHAPTER XL

THE NAKED TRUTH

ALTHOUGH Mr. Roscoe had the *entrée* to Grace's bower, as he had to her sisters', a visit from him, in her case, was by no means such a matter of course. His knock at her boudoir door, with the announcement of his name, in reply to a somewhat severe 'Who is that?'— in a tone that is used by one who is engaged in some occupation not agreeable, but in which he does not wish to be disturbed—did not receive the ready 'Pray come in,' that he had been favoured with on the two previous instances. He was kept waiting at the door time enough to note the circumstance; moreover, when the permission to enter was given, it did not escape him that it was in a despondent voice. Grace indeed had been crying, as he saw at a glance, and also the reason of it, for although she had put away Mr. Allerton's letter, its envelope still lay on the table.

'I wish to have a few words with you, Grace, if you please.' He never addressed her thus familiarly unless the subject was of an importance that seemed to excuse it.

She bowed, and motioned him to a chair. Her silence, as he rightly judged, was compulsory; she could not trust herself to speak.

'I am afraid you have had bad news this morning,' he murmured sympathetically.

'Nothing to speak of,' she answered coldly —so coldly indeed that the tone seemed almost to imply, 'nothing to speak of to *you*; it is my own affair.'

'I deeply regret it,' he answered gently, 'and the more so since I am myself—most unwillingly, as you may be sure—the bearer of evil tidings. But perhaps I have been anticipated,' and he looked significantly at the envelope.

'You mean the letter I have just received from Mr. Allerton? No, there is nothing in it of which I was not aware before.'

'He has heard, I suppose, of your proposed engagement' (she looked up indignantly at that word 'proposed,' as he had known she would, and he kept his own eyes upon the floor), 'and has written to express his dissatisfaction with it. He takes a lawyer's view of it, no doubt; points out you are throwing yourself (by which he means your fortune) away in marrying one forbidden by your father's will. If he has no argument to use but that, he might have saved his time, and you your six and eightpence. It was my impression that he had written of a more serious obstacle.'

'I do not understand you, Mr. Roscoe—what other obstacle? Not that it matters; nothing that Mr. Allerton or any other person could say could affect the matter of which you speak. Indeed, I would not even listen to it.'

'Quite so,' he answered gravely; 'no one has a right to interfere with your private affairs. Your regard for Mr. Sinclair is a sacred matter—I feel that myself. Let us suppose that what has come to my knowledge—and must needs come to his—affects some one else, not him. If anything I am obliged to tell you seems to chime in with anything he has told you of his previous history, put that aside: judge the whole matter from without, as a mere looker-on, and decide upon it without favour or prejudice. That will be the honestest way of coming to a right decision.'

She looked up at him, less in alarm than scorn, though she *was* alarmed, he saw; what her face expressed besides its fear was a doubt of his being the sort of person to recommend what was right, and especially upon the ground of honesty. The suggestion of this rather assisted him in his present purpose, because it set him against her, and stifled the feeble pity he had felt for her.

'I must go back a little,' he continued, 'to start with, into what to you must seem ancient history—to what happened years ago, when you were a little child.

'A certain man of business in the City, very wealthy, but whose only desire in the world was to increase his store, had a poor cousin in the country, who, with the exception of his own family, was his only relative. They had been boys together at school, and he had perhaps as much regard for him as he was capable of feeling for anything outside his money bags. This cousin applied to him respecting the investment of a few thousands —almost all he had in the world—and the other gave him his advice. It was the most that he was ever known to give to anybody, and indeed it was generally of value. When

I say "gave," however, it was never given for nothing. He was by trade a money-lender—a skinflint, or rather a skin-diamond, for he seldom concerned himself with any client who could not directly or indirectly (though more often the latter) repay him handsomely for his services. In the case of his cousin, however, he charged him nothing (at first), and recommended him an investment which, though speculative, he had every reason to believe would turn out to be exceedingly profitable. It was, if I remember right (but this can be easily certified), a certain mine in Cornwall. The money-lender indeed thought so well of it that he had placed a sum to which the other's contribution (though it was, as I have said, his all) was a mere bagatelle in the speculation, himself. As time went on the mine ceased to perform the promise it had given, and its shares fell lower and lower in the market till they almost became valueless. Then the man in the country, grievously alarmed, as he well might be, wrote to his kinsman for his advice again. "I am sure you did the best for me you could," he said, "and indeed must have lost your own money. Of course I have not a word of reproach to write, but I am well-nigh ruined, so be so good as to dispose of these unhappy shares for me at whatever they realise. I am resolved to go to America, there to endeavour to make a livelihood for my wife and son, which is denied them here." It was a pathetic letter (I read it with my own eyes), and almost touched the money-lender, but not quite. He knew more about the mine than anyone else, except its manager, who was in his pay, and had privately given him news that a lode of great extent had just been discovered in it. Without an expenditure of sixpence, and by merely telling his cousin to "hold on," he could have made a fortune for him; but the temptation of adding some thousands, at the price of a few pounds, to his ill-gotten gains, was too strong for him; he wrote to the poor cousin, saying that the shares were unsaleable, but that for the sake of old times, and because the same blood ran in his veins (for there was nothing on earth that the man did not make subservient to his own aggrandisement), he would purchase them himself for, I think (but this also can be ascertained, no doubt), for 300*l*. The offer was accepted; the cousin emigrated with his wife and son on the proceeds of the transaction, and the money-lender within twelve months made 20,000*l*. by it.'

'What has this hateful act by this wicked man to do with me?' inquired Grace defiantly.

'Nothing. You hear of it of course for the first time; but let me conclude my story. The cousin by some means or other learnt how he had been cheated, and told the story to his son, without, however (as I have good reason to believe, though I cannot understand his reticence), revealing the name of the relative who had robbed him. The result of that robbery was that the mother, succumbing to fatigues and privations, died soon after, and the father, after a hard and wretched life, was slain by Indians ; the son———'

He paused, and looked at Grace with keen significance. Her face was white as death ; but there was a fire in her eyes and in her tone, as she exclaimed, ' Go on.'

' The son, I am grieved to say, Grace, is Walter Sinclair, and the man who robbed his father was *your* father.'

' You lie ! ' she thundered. ' My father was the best and kindest of men.'

' Was he ? Ask your friend, Mr. Allerton —*he* knows. Ask Lord Morella who was the money-lender who caught his son, Lord Cheribert, in his meshes, and stripped him of thousands ? Ask your sisters, and they will tell you what everybody else is aware of except yourself, that the man who thus made gold his idol, and sacrificed his kinsman to it (as he had sacrificed hundreds of others), was no other than Joseph Tremenhere.'

Of the last part of this speech Grace had no knowledge; she had thrown up her arms before it was concluded, and with a piteous cry of desolation and despair had fallen on the ground in a dead faint. Under such circumstances man, unless he is medical, is generally useless and inclined to run away, but Mr. Roscoe was not an ordinary specimen of his sex; moreover, even had he preferred 'absence of body to presence of mind,' the apprehension of what she might say to other ears on coming to herself kept him in the path of duty. He lifted her up in his strong arms and placed her on the sofa, from which he removed the pillow, and sprinkling a little water on her face from the jug in the next room, which he did not scruple to enter, awaited events with a philosophical mind. Grace did not come to herself for some minutes, and when she did so still remained with closed eyes, only too conscious doubtless of whom she would behold should she open them.

'Does Walter know?' were her first words.

'No, dear Grace, of course not,' answered her companion comfortingly. 'I came here to spare you that; but of course he must be put in possession of the facts sooner or later. From what I have heard of his devotion to the memory of his father, what has come to light is a thing that he can never forget or forgive. Of course you had nothing to do with it, but there is the sentiment, you see.'

She put up her hand as if in appeal for silence.

'You feel that yourself, I'm sure. It is only too obvious that all between you and him must be over. There is no need to mention the real cause to anybody—not to Mr. Allerton, for instance; but only to your sisters, and even that is only as you please. Trust to me to arrange this unhappy matter so as to give you—and indeed Walter also—as little pain as possible. You will find no doubt in the letter you received this morning an excuse that will satisfy the outside world.' Her hand moved feebly in the direction of the door. 'You wish to be left alone. No doubt that is your wisest course. This is a thing to be thought about and not talked about, even with one who has your interests so near at heart as I have. But I need scarcely impress upon you that there is only one course to be pursued. If you could make the effort, it would save a world of distress and pain to both of you if you would give me a few words in writing just to authorise me to act for you as regards Walter. Write, for instance, "Seek not to see me. Mr. Roscoe will tell you all," and sign it. That will be quite sufficient.' He pushed the writing materials that lay upon the table close to her hand, and she feebly raised herself, and with a dazed, despairing look obeyed him.

'That's a brave girl. Do not hate me, Grace, for the part I have been obliged to play in this miserable business,' and with that he left her.

She tottered to the door, locked it, and then sank into a chair. Except that her position was one of utter misery, for the moment she hardly realised it. She had fallen from the highest rung of the ladder of human happiness on the stones of blank despair. An hour ago she had possessed everything that fortune could give her, and now she was a beggar whose wretchedness no alms could repair. She had already lost her father, and it had been a bitter trial to her, but she had now lost him again in a far more dreadful manner. Would she had never known him at all! To think how she had loved him—yes, and he her; had she not been his 'pet,' his 'joy,' his 'little fairy'?—

and all in vain—or as it seemed in vain; for she had in truth been loving another father, shaped out of her own childish imagination, and with whom this real one had nothing in common. She had no doubt now of her wretched and irretrievable error. A hundred evidences of what had been his calling, though not one of them had witnessed against him before, crowded on her mind. And even still—there was the pity of it—she loved him. An oppressor of the needy, one who took advantage of the necessities of his fellow-creatures, and an unfair advantage—a thief, a thief, a thief!—and yet she loved him still.

Her Walter too was lost for ever—a thought sufficient of itself to make death a boon (ah! if she could but die!); but for the moment even that thought was overwhelmed by the spectacle of what had been the idol of her life shattered in fragments before her, with its front of brass and feet of clay!

CHAPTER XLI

RICHARD TO THE RESCUE

'As easy as lying,' is a common proverb, but it must have been invented by an optimist; one might just as well say 'As easy as writing fiction,' which is not such a facile thing as those who have not tried it are apt to imagine. Mr. Edward Roscoe was a past master in the art of 'making the thing that is not as the thing that is,' but now and then even he found it a difficult job. When he left Grace Tremenhere's boudoir, the perspiration stood upon his brow, so severe had been his exertion in that way, though indeed he had not been exactly lying, but only what doctors and prize-fighters call 'putting on flesh' as regarded what was a very genuine skeleton of fact. The task that lay before him now seemed simple in comparison with that severe operation, for it is so much easier to deal with a man, where the affections are concerned, than with a woman, and his next 'call'—as ruinous as that of a broken bank on its unhappy shareholders—was on Walter Sinclair. Most men in his position would at least have taken that stolen document out of his breast-pocket, and either destroyed it or put it in some place of safety, before seeking an interview with its rightful owner; but Mr. Roscoe's heart was furnished with the triple brass of the poet, and indeed there was a great amount of the same material in the whole of his composition.

He found Walter at his desk busily engaged on some subject connected with his future work, 'plan, elevation, and section,' drawn by rule and line; a miracle of mechanical neatness to which Mr. Roscoe paid his little tribute of admiration before entering on the matter in hand.

'How I envy you your dexterity!' he observed. 'I am so clumsy with my fingers myself that such work as yours looks like magic. I am sorry to interrupt it, but the fact is I have got some bad news for you, which does not admit of delay.'

'Bad news!' exclaimed Walter, throwing down pencil and compass, and looking up at him with some suspicion as well as alarm, which the other did not fail to note.

'Yes; it is bad news, but believe me, I am only the unwilling bringer of it, and not the cause.'

'From whom do you come then?'

'From Miss Grace. Here are my credentials.'

Walter took the strip of paper, and read in what he knew was her hand, though the writing was blurred and trembling—' Seek not to see me. Mr. Roscoe will tell you all.—Grace Tremenhere.'

'Great heaven!' he said, 'what is the meaning of this?'

'The meaning is that she bids you farewell—that all is over between you.'

'It is false!' cried Walter passionately.

Mr. Roscoe shrugged his shoulders. 'It is her writing, not mine,' he said. 'She chose me for the duty I am compelled to perform. You may add to its unpleasantness by insulting me, but I shall perform it all the same.'

'Say what you have got to say, sir, though I will never believe that she told you to say it.'

'That's a matter which—if you don't mind her breaking her heart—you can learn from her own lips, but she was in hopes that for the sake of all that has passed between you, you would spare her.'

'Go on!' exclaimed the young man fiercely.

'The person against whom your passion should be directed, if it must have an object,' continued Mr. Roscoe, 'is your friend, Mr. Allerton. He has discovered, I know not how, that you have been paying your attentions to Miss Grace, and a letter has come to her from him this morning. So much I know of myself. What the letter contains I have learnt only from her. He is her guardian and trustee, you know.'

'I know *that*,' put in the other impatiently.

'Well, since that is the case, he has a right, not indeed to dispose of her hand, but to see the disposal of it does not involve the loss of her fortune. It is his simple duty, and one in aid of which he could, and would, invoke the law.'

'That is not true,' replied Walter; 'I mean as regards the loss of her fortune. She told me so with her own lips.'

'I think you must be mistaken there,' said

Mr. Roscoe mildly. 'She could not have said that, because she is acquainted with the terms of her father's will.'

'She did not say so in so many words; but she told me, when I spoke of the gulf that existed between us as regards disparity of fortune, that there was no such gulf.'

Mr. Roscoe smiled a pitying smile.

'She was right there, my poor fellow. If she married you there would indeed be no such disparity, because by doing so she would have lost her fortune. It was love that caused her so to express herself; I do not deny for a moment that she loves you. We all know it, and in our love for her we were all willing that she should sacrifice her all, because we felt that in that sacrifice she would find her happiness. We are not lawyers, nor her trustees and guardians, as Mr. Allerton is. It is just possible (though I have a better opinion of you) that even now, in the teeth of his opposition (which, however, will be very formidable, I promise you), you may press your suit. But would it be honourable, would it become anyone calling himself a man, to take advantage of the simplicity and affection of a young girl under such circumstances, even if she were prepared to give up what is nothing less than a huge fortune, and to accept a life of poverty for your sake—and I honestly tell you that she is not so prepared, and sends me here to tell you so? Would you take her on such terms? If I know you, Walter Sinclair, as the son of an honest man, and an honest man yourself, you would not so take her.'

Walter turned from his companion, and with his elbows on the desk, and his face hidden in his hands, uttered one solitary groan, the knell of his bright hopes.

'Of course it is a terrible trial to you; but it was a worse one to her. The struggle between love and duty is always a cruel one; but Grace is duty itself. She idolised

her father, and what he expressly forbad (as
Mr. Allerton pointed out to her) she repents
of having been about to do. You loved and
respected *your* father, Walter; would *you* not
hesitate to disobey his last solemn injunctions? I think you would.'

'Stop! there is something wrong here,'
exclaimed the young man suddenly, rising
slowly from his seat, and confronting his
companion with so keen a glance that it
needed all his hardihood to meet it coolly.
'When we were on the river this summer
Lord Cheribert was with us. He was himself
in love with Grace (how indeed could he
help it, poor fellow!). Everyone knows it
as well as I, except perhaps Grace herself;
Mr. Allerton knew it, and if, as you say—
but I forgot, he was a wealthy man.'

'Just so,' said Mr. Roscoe persuasively.
('Thank heaven, this fool has never looked
at Josh's will for himself,' was his inward
reflection.) 'Or, if he was not wealthy,

he had vast expectations. He would have brought as much as he found. There were not the same objections to him as in your case, though there *were* objections.'

'Nevertheless I must see her,' exclaimed Walter desperately. 'There may be some way of escape, some loophole. Or the whole thing may be a mistake, a plot. You villain, you dog!' he cried, seizing the other by his coat-collar (within an inch of where the secret lay), 'if this is any plan of yours to part us, I will have your heart's blood.'

'Be so good as to unhand me, sir, for my own temper is somewhat short,' said Mr. Roscoe resolutely. 'This is scarcely the reward one looks to for breaking bad news to a fellow-creature. Go to Grace then, by all means, and put the finishing stroke to Mr. Allerton's morning's work. Only if it kills her, sir, it will be no less than murder.'

'Go, go, or there will be murder *here*!'

exclaimed the young man furiously, and throwing open the door he thrust the other from the room, slammed the door behind him, and locked himself in. The whole thing did not take a minute, but it was full of 'action.' The impression on Mr. Roscoe's mind, though not upon his body, was that he had been *kicked* out.

'I will be even with you for this, my man,' was what he muttered to himself with lips pale with rage, though, if he could have looked at matters with an unprejudiced eye, the obligation still lay upon the other side.

Left to his own maddening thoughts, Walter Sinclair sat at his desk, with that scrap in Grace's handwriting spread out before him, 'Seek not to see me. Mr. Roscoe will tell you all,' examining it with the anxious scrutiny one might have bestowed upon a cryptogram, who is conscious of a lack of clearness in his mind necessary for its elucidation. The words indeed were plain enough, and their meaning had been explained to him with sufficient distinctness, but was it the true meaning? Upon the whole he was forced to the conclusion that it was. If it was a lie, one line from Allerton, not to mention one word from Grace's lips, would, as Roscoe must be well aware, have confuted it. His arguments indeed had from a worldly point of view been overwhelming. Curst be the gold that is weighed in the scales with true love, but it kicks the beam. To Grace's guardian and trustee it could not seem otherwise, nor did he blame him; he only blamed the gold. With Grace herself he knew it had no such weight; but that very fact, as Roscoe had pointed out, should prevent him from pressing his suit. Her simplicity and ignorance, her girlish contempt for the gifts of fortune, were only apparent allies; it would be cowardly to take advantage of them even if he could bring himself to do so; then there were her father's last injunctions which in her new-found love she had perhaps forgotten till the lawyer had reminded her of them. He had vaguely heard that Mr. Tremenhere had made his fortune as a money-lender, a circumstance that had in no way affected him. He might have been a good man for all that; that he had been a loving father to Grace was certain, and she had reciprocated his love with all the warmth of her nature. He was himself devoted to his father's memory, and, as Roscoe had cunningly surmised, that circumstance had great weight with him; he put himself in Grace's place, and sided with her, as it were, against himself.

Still to part with him without a word of farewell seemed unnatural, hard, and cruel, and utterly foreign to Grace's nature. True there was her handwriting before him, 'Seek not to see me.' The question was, by what process had those words been wrung from her? If she had written them of her own free will, his duty was plain: he must pack up his things and leave Halswater Hall at once.

When he had gone away—whither he could not tell; all places seemed alike to him, and all hateful—he would write and wish her farewell. She could reply to him or not, as she pleased. He staggered into his bedroom, and began putting his clothes together with blind haste. While thus occupied he heard a violent knock at his sitting-room door.

'Who is it?' he asked hoarsely.

'It is I, Richard Roscoe. Open.'

To see anyone just then was a trial he was ill-fitted to undergo; the thought of an interview with this man, half mad as he believed him to be, and wholly unfitted to sympathise with such a calamity as had befallen him, was especially distasteful to him.

'I am busy,' he called out.

'No matter,' was the impatient reply, 'I must see you.' And again came the loud summons at the door.

Fearing that the servants would be alarmed, and a disturbance created, when it was so necessary that anything of the kind should be avoided, he opened the door, and a moment afterwards repented of it.

Richard Roscoe stood before him, his face white and wet, his hair dishevelled, his eyes rolling in what seemed like frenzy, and, in a word, more like a madman than he had ever seen him. He entered hastily, and at once relocked the door.

'Don't be afraid of me,' he said in breathless tones, as though he had perceived what was passing through the other's mind; 'I am not mad, though I have heard enough to make me so. What are you doing here? Packing up? I thought so. What is that paper in Grace's hand?'

In one stride he had reached the desk and read her words.

'How dare you?' exclaimed Walter passionately.

'Sir, I dare anything for Grace's sake,' was the unexpected rejoinder. "Mr. Roscoe will tell you all," she says, but she does not know the man as his brother does. "Seek not to see me." But you *shall* see her. Sit down, Walter Sinclair, and listen to *me*.'

CHAPTER XLII

THE BROTHERS

AFTER the unpleasant parting Mr. Edward Roscoe had had with Walter Sinclair, it might have seemed probable that he would have had enough of interviews for the day; but not only was his brother Richard, to whom he had also a word or two to say, under the same roof and close at hand, but the very violence with which he had been treated in the one case was a spur to him in the other. His anger against the young man was very great, and, as it happened, the communication he had to make to Richard comprehended in it the greatest blow to Walter's hopes that could possibly be struck, 'which,' as a greater hypocrite than even Mr. Roscoe has observed before him, 'was very soothing.' He had no doubt, in spite of the self-restraint his brother had used in his relations with Grace, that his feeling towards her remained unchanged, and also that, notwithstanding his apparent friendship with her lover, he in reality regarded him with all the disfavour of an unsuccessful rival. Though far from falling into the error of less sagacious scoundrels in judging his fellow-creatures by himself, Mr. Roscoe was incapable of understanding such a virtue as magnanimity.

It was, in fact, in a tone which honestly expressed his convictions that as soon as he had entered his brother's room he observed with cheerful gravity:

'Richard, my lad, I have got some good news for you!'

'Indeed!' answered Richard bitterly, as he rose from his seat to greet him, and put down the book he had been reading, 'then it must be very strange news.'

'It *is* strange news, my good fellow—stranger than anything you can have imagined, better than anything you can have dreamt of! Sit down and listen to it, for it will make your limbs tremble under you with joy. The engagement between Grace and Walter Sinclair has been broken off.'

'What?' Only a word, only a monosyllable, but what a tumult of emotions—hope and love and pity and amazement—did it express! The very face of the man was transfigured with them.

'Yes, it is as true as death. The whole thing is over; Grace is now fancy free—is at all events free to have a fancy for someone else. There is now a chance for *you*, man!'

Richard looked at him with wondering eyes; he was so full indeed of astonishment that he was unable to take in the whole situation as it was thus suddenly presented to him. He did not even catch the meaning of his brother's words, which could certainly not have been from their want of distinctness. His mind could hardly grasp the stupendous fact that had been disclosed to him, far less its probable consequences.

'Have they quarrelled?' he inquired in a hoarse whisper.

'I am happy to say they have not, for we all know what lovers' quarrels end in. The thing goes far deeper than that. You may take my word for it that they will never see each other again.'

Mr. Edward Roscoe's word was a guarantee beyond suspicion to almost everybody at Halswater Hall, but (doubtless because of the eccentricity of Richard's character) his brother seemed to doubt it; nay, with a frankness that, however common in the Western wilds. is unusual in polite society, he coldly replied, 'I don't believe you, Edward. It is only because you have some end of your own to serve that you wish to make me credit such an incredible statement.'

'A very natural supposition, my dear Dick,' answered the other cheerfully, 'and one that does honour to your intelligence; but you have only to step across the passage into Walter's room to get the matter certified. I wouldn't do it just now, if I were you, because he's rather upset about it; there will be plenty of time before he starts, though I suppose he will be off this afternoon.'

'Do you mean to say he is leaving Halswater?'

'Well, I conclude he is. From what I have told you, you will see for yourself that no other course is open to him.'

'How did it come about?' inquired Richard.

'Well, it was all through Mr. Allerton. He is her guardian, and has forbidden the banns, as he has the power to do. If she had had any sense she would have married Walter at once, and then written to the lawyer to say so; but he has somehow discovered her engagement, and put his foot down on it. She will be wiser next time, Dick, you may take your oath of that.'

'And she has given him up because the lawyer tells her to do so?'

'I don't say that exactly; there are other reasons I am bound in honour not to go into, and which you must not press me about. But what is the main thing—as concerns yourself—the match is broken off.'

'Poor lad, poor lad!'

'Well, of course one is sorry for him, but one must look after oneself in this world. It is an ill wind that blows nobody good, and without your having any hand in it, without your having the least thing to reproach yourself with, a good opportunity has opened to you. I suppose, though you did what you could to smother your affection for the young woman, the cinders of it are still alive?'

'I love Grace—oh, yes, I love her still!' murmured Richard softly.

'That's right. You have a faithful heart, I know, Dick. So have I, though the object of its desire may be a little different. We both stick to our views. It runs in the family. Well, you know what I told you of the reason that first caused me to write you to come home from America. Circumstances did away with that reason for the time, but it has now sprung to life again. I had a matrimonial engagement for you in my mind, which I must confess is a merely practical one; the idea never entered into it that the young woman I designed for you would become the girl of your heart, but fortunately it has so turned out. A few hours ago she was altogether out of your reach, now she has come within it; you have only to put your arms about her, though I need not say that must be done in a most cautious and delicate fashion. At first of course she will be inconsolable for the loss of her first love; but little by little the gilt of sentiment will be rubbed off, and half a loaf—if I may say so without offence, for you are really neither so young nor so good-looking as Sinclair—will seem better than no bread.'

'I see,' said Richard gently (he had his hands before his eyes, and seemed lost in thought), then added with effort, like one rousing himself from sleep, 'What would you have me do?'

'Just now, nothing. What I would recommend for the present is a " masterly inaction"; bide your time, by which of course I mean your opportunity; sooner or later it is sure to come. Be as gentle and sympathising with the girl as you please, but do not drop a word of love. She will want something to cling to, and in due course that should be you. There will be objections to you, as there were to Sinclair, on the lawyer's part, no doubt, but she will not sacrifice her happiness a second time for a mere sentiment, which by then moreover will have grown weaker. Upon the whole,' concluded Mr. Roscoe cheerfully, 'I really believe this misfortune, as it first seemed to us, will turn out but a blessing in disguise.'

'It is very good of you to take such an interest in my affairs,' observed Richard.

His brother glanced up at him very sharply, but there was nothing to be read on the other's face but a settled gloom.

'Blood is thicker than water, my lad,' answered Edward. 'It will give me unfeigned pleasure to see you comfortably settled in life; but I must frankly add that it will be also advantageous to myself. As Grace's husband you will be one of the family, and I shall be able to arrange matters with you much more easily than with a stranger—such as Sinclair for example. I shall feel easier in my mind, by the bye, when that young gentleman is out of the house.'

'You are sure that he will not insist upon seeing Grace before he takes his departure?'

'That is quite settled. To do him justice, he acknowledged, when I pointed it out to him, that it would be a most selfish act, and only give her unnecessary pain : it would also (which I did not point out to him) be a most dangerous experiment.'

'You mean to our interests?'

'Well, of course in the presence of the once beloved object she might lose sight of her obvious duty. She has made up her mind to perform it, and it would be madness to give him the chance of shaking her resolution. He too has come to the same decision. But if he could be persuaded to be off, without seeing any member of the family, it would be a great point gained. He is attached to you, and has not the least suspicion of your feelings towards Grace ; it would be well if you could persuade him to leave at once. You can tell him that I will gladly explain matters for him to Agnes and Philippa.'

'I will,' said Richard decisively.

'That's a good fellow. In the meantime, while you are getting him away, I will see that all is safe in the other quarter. Use all the arguments you can think of, and remember that you are now taking the first step on the road to your happiness. When I next see you I hope we shall have the cottage to ourselves,' and with that he left the room.

Notwithstanding the readiness with which he had fallen in with his brother's suggestion, Richard did not at once proceed upon his promised errand. He stood with his eyes closed and his hands clasped tightly before him; his lips moved as if in prayer, and the words, 'Deliver us from temptation,' fell from them in broken tones. If his brother could have seen him, he would certainly have said, 'This man is mad,' yet even so perhaps would not have deemed him too mad to marry.

'Walter, Walter!' he murmured to himself pitifully, and then in still tenderer tones, 'Grace, Grace!' The struggle within him, as it showed itself in his face, was terrible to witness; now his better nature and now his worse seemed to be getting the upper hand; at last the former triumphed, but with so great difficulty, with such a dead lift of all his powers for good, that he could not trust himself to let the debate begin again. He ran out of the room and knocked at Walter's door, crying 'Open, open!' Despair was in his heart, but from every thought of baseness it had been swept clean.

CHAPTER XLIII

METHOD IN HIS MADNESS

THOUGH the look and manner of Richard Roscoe were so strange and wild, there was a fervour and earnestness in the tone in which he said, 'Sit down and I will tell you all,' that commanded Sinclair's attention; even a madman may have a story to tell that has nothing to do with his own state of mind, and may have pith and moment in it.

'You see before you an unfortunate man,' he began, 'but not a rogue and a liar; you may trust me—yes, you may trust me now—as your father trusted me before; you may say indeed to his own undoing, but that was owing to no fault of mine, but to human weakness, and you have heard the worst of it from my own lips.'

'I do not think you were to blame in that matter,' said Walter gently; 'if you were so, though it was a dreadful business, you have my full forgiveness, as I am sure you had that of my poor father.'

'I thank you for saying so, my lad, with all my heart. With such words in my ears I should be a villain indeed were I to play you false. It is not a pleasant thing to have to say that one's own mother's son is a rascal, but there is no help for it but to confess as much; my brother Edward is one of that sort. He has been so from his cradle. Yes, Heaven knows I have tried to think otherwise, though I have had proof enough to the contrary. It seems an unnatural and ungrateful thing to speak, when I am at this moment sharing the roof and eating the bread that his good offices have obtained for me. And let me tell you, Walter Sinclair, he has promised me much more—a reward so great that I dare not even think of it—if I will only join him in his cursed plans and help to accomplish your ruin!'

'My ruin?' cried Walter in astonishment.

'Yes, what else? To tear you from her you love, to take away the only object from you that serves to make life worth the living, to drive you out of Paradise into a barren land, where not a flower grows nor a bird sings, and the sun itself only rises to show you your own wretchedness—is not *that* ruin?'

'It is indeed,' groaned Walter; 'I have been face to face with it for what seems an eternity, the last hour.'

'Well, that shall not be. Had I been in your case no power on earth would have made me believe that those words written by Grace's hand came from her heart.'

'But your brother——'

'Still less would I have believed *his*

words,' broke in the other contemptuously.
'You did not know him, it is true, as I know
him, but you knew *her*, and how could you
think even for an instant that the advice of a
lawyer or the reflection that she should lose
money by it—were it millions—would cause
that angelic nature to break her plighted
word and forsake the man she loves?'

'It is not the money, Richard—though
that has weight with me, though not with
her—nor the arguments of her guardian; it
is " the dead hand " that has turned her from
me, the last injunction of a loving father.'

'That is what Edward told you, did he?'
answered Richard bitterly. 'He said there
were other reasons for which I must not press.
His delicacy of mind was always extraordinary, though he forgot it for a moment
in taking it for granted that I was even a
greater scoundrel than himself. I don't believe his story. There is at all events some
huge lie at the bottom of his mountain of

words; there always is, if you dig deep enough. I am here to help you to dig.'

'I am infinitely obliged to you,' said Walter hoarsely; 'only show me where to put the spade in.'

'Well, to begin with, stop where you are till you find there are real grounds for your departure, and, above all, take no dismissal save from Grace's own lips.'

'She says, "Seek not to see me,"' answered Walter piteously. 'I love her too dearly to disobey her.'

'She does *not* say it, she *writes* it,' answered Richard confidently, 'which is a very different thing. I have known men, captive in Indian hands, compelled to write things to their friends quite other than what their hearts dictated, yet their end, poor souls, was all the same; and so it will be with Grace, if you give way to this wretched scruple. When he has his point to gain Edward is an Indian—subtle, treacherous, and, though not delighting, as they do, in the torture they inflict, utterly callous to it. Somehow or other—I have not his wits, and cannot read his brain, but I know *the man* —somehow or other Grace Tremenhere has become his captive; his net is round her— she is beating her tender wings against it, poor soul, poor soul!—but his will is her will, and these words his words. If such a stake were worth speaking of, I would lay my life upon it.'

The rude eloquence of his words were backed by an earnestness and conviction that would have made their way to any heart, even had it harboured no such desire to be convinced as Walter's did.

'I will stay here till Grace tells me to go,' he said. 'How can I ever thank you enough for bringing me this ray of hope?'

'You never can,' was the grave rejoinder. 'Thank Heaven that sent me here instead. Remain in your room, whatever happens, till

I come back with tidings of how the land lies. Budge for nobody, and least of all for my brother; he has no more right to give you notice to quit the Hall than I have. No one has any right to do it save Grace only.'

It was strange to see one so eccentric thus dictating a course of action to another of sane mind, and so it struck Walter himself; but when we desire anything very much we are not solicitous to inquire closely into the capacity or the motives of those who volunteer their assistance to us. The notion of any plot having been devised against him had never entered Walter's head, but, once there, it filled him with an indignation that would have astonished the plotter. A generous and impulsive nature is easily imposed upon, but having discovered that it has been so, it often becomes more dangerous to deal with than a more calculating one. It has a wrong to humanity to avenge as well as its private wrong—a sentiment which is absolutely unintelligible to the mere scoundrel. It was fortunate perhaps for all parties, but certainly for Mr. Edward Roscoe, that his impatience to see Walter out of the house did not urge him to pay that young gentleman another visit till some time had elapsed after Richard's revelation to him. When he did come, 'Bradshaw' in hand, Walter had cooled down, and was found, though with a somewhat trembling hand, engaged as before upon his plan-drawing.

'You have not much time to lose, my good fellow,' said his visitor with friendly solicitude, 'if you want, as I conclude, to catch the night mail. I have ordered the dogcart to be round in twenty minutes.'

'I am sorry that you should have troubled yourself, Mr. Roscoe, but if I go to-day it will only be to my old quarters at the head of the lake, and I should not go even so far as that without saying good-bye to Grace.'

'Not surely after her expressed wish that

you should not seek to see her, Mr. Sinclair?' answered the other, in a tone of mild astonishment that suited ill with his knitted brow.

'Yes, I remember what she wrote perfectly well, but I intend to hear that wish from her own lips. It is possible that I may have given you a contrary impression. I have also heard all your brother had to say upon the subject; but I have been thinking over the matter since, and that is the resolution to which I have come. And it is not to be broken.'

'Nothing, Mr. Sinclair, but your youth and inexperience can excuse such a conclusion,' observed the other calmly. 'It is an outrage upon hospitality, to say the least of it. You will compel me to ask Miss Agnes herself to give you your *congé*.'

'I shall not take it even from her, but only from Grace herself.'

'Then you will at least take the consequences,' exclaimed Mr. Roscoe furiously, 'for in that case I will have you turned out by the servants.'

'You have dropped your mask, however,' replied Walter coolly—though indeed the other's face had lost its natural expression and *become* a mask, with rage and malignity painted upon it—'which saves me all further circumlocution, at which I am at such a disadvantage with you. As for turning me out, I possess a revolver, and if any violence is offered to me I shall look upon you as the instigator, and give you its contents. You will have the "first chance," as the lawyer said to the mortgagee.'

As the other stood silent for a moment, and menacing, as a volcano before its outbreak, Agnes was seen to hurry by, crying out, 'Mr. Roscoe, Mr. Roscoe!'

He threw open the door at once—not sorry, perhaps, to have his interview cut short. 'I am here; what is the matter?'

'I am afraid Grace is very ill,' she answered excitedly. 'Philippa and I can do nothing with her.'

Walter came forward to the door. The flush of anger had passed from his face, which now only showed anxiety and alarm.

For the moment Agnes forgot his changed relations with her sister, and with womanly sympathy observed :

'Yes, indeed, she is very ill, Walter. The doctor should be sent for at once, Mr. Roscoe.'

'To be sure. I will order Saltfish to be saddled at once ; she will do the five miles in twenty minutes. Perhaps Mr. Sinclair himself would like to go.'

'By all means,' Walter was about to say, but a glance at the other's Mephistophelean face prevented it; he remembered too Richard's last injunction, ' Budge for nobody, and least of all for Edward,' and was not this Edward's advice ?

'No, no!' put in Agnes quickly. 'The

mare is queer-tempered and must have one she knows for her rider. Tell Charles to go.'

Mr. Roscoe turned away at once to obey her.

Having received no instructions from her domestic adviser as to giving him his *congé*, Agnes would, as Walter sagely judged, be open to reason.

'With sickness in a house, Miss Agnes,' he said softly, 'it is generally advisable for the "stranger within its gates" to depart. But being at the cottage here, it is impossible that I should be in anybody's way. Under the circumstances, therefore, I must ask your leave to remain where I am till I am assured of dear Grace's safety.'

Perhaps Walter's youth and good looks pleaded for him, though she had a suspicion that his presence would be unwelcome to Mr. Roscoe, or perhaps Grace's illness touched her woman's heart. She hesitated, and looked round as if for advice, but Mr. Edward was in the stable yard and out of reach, and in the end nature had her way.

'Your request does not appear to me unreasonable, Mr. Sinclair,' she replied—then added more doubtfully, 'So far as I am concerned, of course you are very welcome to my hospitality.'

'Then no one else has a right to deny it to me,' said Walter quickly.

This was imprudent, because it suggested the very obstacle Agnes had in her mind.

'That is so,' she answered; 'still, circumstances may arise—— What is it, Mr. Richard?'

Richard Roscoe was approaching from the Hall, evidently in a state of great excitement. 'What is it?' he echoed vehemently. 'Merely that you are, amongst you, trying to send to heaven before her time the sweetest soul that ever dwelt in human form. Philippa tells me that Grace is in a high fever, and does not recognise you as her sisters—not, Heaven knows, that *that* is any proof of madness!'

'You must be mad yourself to say so,' exclaimed Agnes with indignation. 'I shall certainly acquaint your brother with the language you have thought fit to use to me.'

'He may murder me if he likes, but he shall not murder Grace,' cried Richard. 'I know the temptation is very great to all of you. You want to divide by two instead of by three.'

'What, in Heaven's name, does the man mean?' asked Agnes, addressing herself to Walter.

'*He* doesn't know,' continued Richard scornfully; 'but my cunning brother knows, and I think *you* know. You will tell him what I say, and get the house cleared of me as well as of Sinclair. Then you will have Grace all to yourselves to do as you please with, and there will be murder done.'

'If there is enough sanity in this man to make it worth while to note his words at all,' said Agnes with dignity, 'I call upon you,

Mr. Sinclair, to tell him what I have just said to you: "that you are free to stay here as long as you please."'

'That is so, is it?' said Richard, as Walter bowed in confirmation; 'then here we remain together to keep watch and ward over the innocent, and to take vengeance, if they work their wicked will upon her, against the guilty.'

'There is no one, Richard, who means any harm to dear Grace, I am sure,' said Walter soothingly. 'The doctor has been sent for, and let us hope his report may be more favourable than you imagine.'

'You don't know Indians as I know them,' observed Richard laconically, and with that he entered the cottage and retired to his own room.

'Permit me, Miss Agnes,' said Walter gently, 'to express my sorrow that I should have been compelled, in your presence, to listen to such wild and wandering words. If

I might venture to advise you, I would say, "Let them be forgotten." It is clear that poor Mr. Richard is not himself, though I cannot imagine what has caused him to entertain the monstrous idea to which he has given expression.'

'Nor I,' said Agnes coldly; her anger had not left her, but was rather subsiding. The charge Richard had made against her was most unjust, but it was not absolutely groundless, for that division by two instead of three was a sum Mr. Roscoe had often spoken of to her. Nor was the cause of Richard's excitement, since she knew of his secret love for Grace, so inconceivable to her as she pretended.

CHAPTER XLIV

DIFFICULTIES

THAT nothing happens for certain except the unexpected is a dogma that all of us have to subscribe to. It is proved in small matters as well as in large ones, alike in the case of those who have dramatic experiences or who lead homely and uneventful lives. The inmates of Halswater Hall were no exception to this rule. After the painful scenes and violent quarrels that had lately taken place among them, it would have hardly seemed possible that a week, far less a month, hence, would have found them all living together under the same roof, and, outwardly at least, in the same fashion as before. Yet so it was. The result was brought about by the dangerous illness of Grace Tremenhere. When, after her interview with Mr. Roscoe, her sisters, alarmed by her absence from the family circle, went to her room, they found her, as has been said, in sad case, and when the Doctor arrived he gave a most serious report of her.

'Your sister,' he said, 'is suffering from the effect of some severe shock to her system. I do not wish to be intrusive, but it is absolutely necessary for the proper treatment of her case that I should know what has happened.'

Dr. Gardner (as he was always called, though he was only a general practitioner) was by no means of the ordinary type of country doctor. He had an independence of his own, and practised medicine because he liked it. He was highly esteemed in the county, and, what is very rare with men of his profession, was on the bench of magistrates. It is probable that Mr. Roscoe would not have sent for him if the services of a more pliant practitioner could have been procured on equally short notice, but there was no time to pick and choose. Moreover, it was not Mr. Roscoe, but the two ladies to whom he was addressing himself. His countenance, a fine florid one, looked so grave behind his moon-shaped spectacles, that they did not venture to deny the conclusion to which his professional observation had led him. Philippa indeed was so frightened that if she had been alone she would probably have given him every detail; but when the two sisters were together the elder was always the speaker.

'The engagement between my sister and Mr. Sinclair, of which you have doubtless heard,' said Agnes, ' has been suddenly broken off.'

'Oh! that's it, is it?' said the Doctor. 'Um! ha! And not, I suppose, by the young lady's own desire?'

'Yes; the disruption is her own act entirely. It is in no respect a family arrangement, if you mean that,' was the brusque reply.

'Nay, I meant nothing of the kind, madam, but only to get at the facts,' returned the Doctor dryly. 'I may take it, I suppose, that her determination, however necessary and unrepented of, has given her pain?'

'No doubt,' exclaimed Philippa, glancing with tearful eyes towards the bed, where Grace was lying with flushed cheeks and wandering speech, 'that is what has done the mischief.'

'To minister to a mind diseased is beyond my skill, Miss Philippa,' observed the Doctor gently, 'but we must do what we can.' He wrote out certain prescriptions, and then said, 'I will send Miss Grace a good nurse.'

'My sister and I are surely the proper persons to attend upon her,' observed Agnes.

'No. Relations are too sympathetic. In a case like this it is most important that there should be nothing to excite the patient. She will be here to-night. I will pay an early visit to-morrow morning.'

There was only one way, it was said in Westmoreland, of evading Dr. Gardner's prescriptions—by dismissal, and Miss Agnes was not prepared to go to that length. She noticed, however, with great displeasure that for the future he preferred to address himself, when giving orders about his patient, to Philippa instead of herself; and though she had had no idea in her mind other than a kind one in preferring to nurse Grace with her own hands, the Doctor's refusal of her request made Richard's wild accusations especially hateful to her.

'That woman's as hard as nails,' was the Doctor's reflection as he rode away. 'My objection to her tending the poor girl because she was too sympathetic was a good one,' by which, as he rolled his head and winked his eye in evident enjoyment of his own

able smoothness, notwithstanding late events.
There was a difference of course, however, in
the manner of their going. In spite of their
dread of the sick room, Agnes and Philippa
were a good deal, by turns, in their sister's
room, and scarcely ever appeared together
in public, even at meals. These were always
melancholy affairs; for many days the Angel
of Death hovered over the household and
laid its finger on every lip. The Doctor, indeed (none of your despairing ones), could
at one time only say, 'I do not yet give up
all hope.' It may be imagined, therefore,
how Walter's spirits sank to zero, and the
gloom darkened on Richard Roscoe's brow;
they found a melancholy consolation in one
another's company, but seldom interchanged
a word. Walter knew that he had Richard's
sympathy, but never guessed the sufferings—so
blind is love to others as well as to its object
—that he endured upon his own account.
Agnes was genuinely grieved, and Philippa

passionately so; her soul was weary with remorse as well as pity. Mr. Roscoe alone was resigned to the obstruction that interfered with his plans, and looked confidently to nature to remove it. He had no ill-will to Grace, he confessed to himself, but it would be a great relief to him if she went to heaven. *Dis aliter visum*, or, as he expressed it, 'this business turned out as badly as every other infernal thing that he had put his hand to.' Grace got better; it was not the worst thing that could have happened to him, but it complicated matters that were already in a very serious tangle. The rejoicings of the household jarred upon him in a manner that, looking at himself from the outside as it was his habit to do, almost alarmed him.

Disappointment and delay he had hitherto borne with wonderful equanimity, considering the dangers they brought with them, but he felt that he was now losing his patience and his temper. As there is nothing so suc-

"yes" or "no" to that question at present. It is only too likely that it may make no difference to the poor girl whether the young man goes or stays; she is on the brink of brain fever. But should she survive it, it would in my opinion be the wiser course to keep Mr. Sinclair—and from what I gather from her sisters I conclude he has no wish to go—within reach. His presence may be of the greatest service; and if the worst comes to the worst, it may be a comfort to her to wish him farewell.'

'With brain fever?' inquired Mr. Roscoe cynically, his disappointment at the other's reply getting the better of his usual self-restraint.

'I am supposing that she comes to herself again,' answered the Doctor harshly, for he too had a temper of his own; 'if not, I presume Miss Tremenhere will not grudge the hospitality she has thrown away upon him. Good afternoon, sir,' and with a curt nod he put spurs to his cob and rode away.

'An impudent apothecary!' was Mr. Roscoe's comment as he turned to enter the house; but, however he may have despised the man, he felt that a spoke had been put into the wheel of his plan, which, for a time at least, would interfere with its working. Even in his anger, however, he clearly perceived the source of this mischance. 'This all comes of the senseless frankness with which that old busybody's questions have been answered upstairs,' he muttered to himself. 'Agnes I can trust not to lose her head, but Philippa, where sentiment is concerned, is always a fool.' He did not feel any especial resentment towards Walter, as a less practical schemer would have done, but, since it was now probable that the young fellow would stay on, resolved to treat him with civility. And thus it happened that things went on at the Hall with tolerable smoothness, notwithstanding late events. There was a difference of course, however, in the manner of their going. In spite of their dread of the sick room, Agnes and Philippa were a good deal, by turns, in their sister's room, and scarcely ever appeared together in public, even at meals. These were always melancholy affairs; for many days the Angel of Death hovered over the household and laid its finger on every lip. The Doctor, indeed (none of your despairing ones), could at one time only say, 'I do not yet give up all hope.' It may be imagined, therefore, how Walter's spirits sank to zero, and the gloom darkened on Richard Roscoe's brow; they found a melancholy consolation in one another's company, but seldom interchanged a word. Walter knew that he had Richard's sympathy, but never guessed the sufferings—so blind is love to others as well as to its object—that he endured upon his own account. Agnes was genuinely grieved, and Philippa passionately so ; her soul was weary with remorse as well as pity. Mr. Roscoe alone was resigned to the obstruction that interfered with his plans, and looked confidently to nature to remove it. He had no ill-will to Grace, he confessed to himself, but it would be a great relief to him if she went to heaven. *Dis aliter visum*, or, as he expressed it, 'this business turned out as badly as every other infernal thing that he had put his hand to.' Grace got better ; it was not the worst thing that could have happened to him, but it complicated matters that were already in a very serious tangle. The rejoicings of the household jarred upon him in a manner that, looking at himself from the outside as it was his habit to do, almost alarmed him.

Disappointment and delay he had hitherto borne with wonderful equanimity, considering the dangers they brought with them, but he felt that he was now losing his patience and his temper. As there is nothing so successful as success, so he was well aware there is nothing that precipitates calamity like desperation, and yet he was growing desperate. He knew it and fought against it, but, though slowly, despair was gaining the upper hand of him. Perils environed him on every side of which no one knew, or knew all, except himself. As Josh had foreseen, and even taxed him with that folly, Edward Roscoe was a gambler to the core; he could perceive the rashness of it in others, with whom it took other directions, and he had often profited by it. He was not even blind to it in his own case, but his overpowering egotism and confidence in his own sagacity had led him into enormous speculations, which had turned out ill, and involved him in liabilities which he had no means of meeting, except by driblets and fair words. He was furious, not so much with his ill luck, as with the failure of his own forecasts. He had been taken in by inferior scoundrels.

If he had had any, one might almost have said that his self-respect was wounded. What helped to drive him to despair was the atmosphere of hate—his own hate, and of his own making—with which he was surrounded. He had never cared for anyone but himself, but that very solicitude had hitherto prevented him from indulging in animosities which are always disadvantageous; he had had, at the worst, only a cold contempt for those who stood in his way or thwarted his schemes. But now he began to hate them. Even his brother, though Agnes had never revealed his conduct to her, had become an object of suspicion to him. He resented his familiarity with Walter, and felt that he was not to be depended upon for carrying out his scheme with respect to Grace. If the girl had died this would not have mattered, but she was getting better. If she got well, and was reconciled, in spite of all that had come and gone, with Walter, it would not matter;

but he was none the less angry with Richard. He now repented that he had made a confidante of either of the sisters with respect to the document that he had intercepted; women were not fit to be trusted with secrets, though at the time it had seemed to him the safest course to take. It was not likely that they would reveal it, since it would be the destruction of their own expectations. If Grace should ever marry Walter she should never know but that she did so otherwise than to her own detriment; he would be always Sinclair to her and never Vernon; though Roscoe now wished that he had kept that matter to himself. But he hated Sinclair because there lay in him—though he knew it not and should never know it—the potentiality of seizing the whole Tremenhere estate for himself or his offspring.

Philippa, indeed, Mr. Roscoe could hardly be said to hate; but he was exasperated with her for her weakness about the young people, which had enlisted the Doctor on their side, and also for a certain obstinacy which she still occasionally exhibited in opposing his wishes. The person he hated most of all was the lady whose hospitality he was enjoying, and who had done him a hundred good offices, Agnes Tremenhere. It is said that the very wickedest of us have a tender spot in our hard hearts for those who love us, that even a Sikes has a weakness for his Nancy. But this is not only not the case, but in some instances their very liking for us aggravates our dislike for them. Perhaps if Agnes had always been subservient to him he would have had the same contemptuous tolerance for her as he had for Philippa, but her occasional fits of fondness found no favour with him; while her opposition, which was much more frequent and resolute than that of her sister, now inspired him with a feeling that was little short of fury. Mr. Edward

Roscoe felt, in short, that he was becoming dangerous; a thing which would not have troubled him much had he not been aware that such a frame of mind was likely to be hurtful not only to others but to himself.

CHAPTER XLV

'EDWARD'S QUEEN'

GRACE TREMENHERE had survived the crisis of what had been a most dangerous illness, and was on the road to recovery; she had returned to consciousness, but yet could hardly have been said to have 'come to herself.' Her condition resembled that of some would-be suicide who, having been rescued from the fate she has sought, says to herself, 'Am I alive, or am I dead?' and then comes suddenly to the sad knowledge that it is the Present—and the Past—that she is confronting, and not the Future.

But the Grace Tremenhere whom we knew she was no longer. Her beautiful hair is shorn, her eyes are caverns, her cheeks are shrunk and pale; but all that is nothing compared with the hopeless void within. The consciousness of the full extent of her misery has come back to her. When she awoke first with a sane mind, it so happened that only the nurse and the Doctor were in the room.

'Is he here still?' she inquired feebly.

'Yes, my dear, he has not gone yet,' said the nurse consolingly. 'Miss Grace is asking for you, sir.'

The Doctor took her place by the bedside. He knew that he was not in the girl's thoughts at all, but that did not wound his *amour propre*. His weather-beaten face was full of the keenest sympathy, yet cheery too; of all his medicines Dr. Gardner was, his patients said, the most wholesome tonic.

'Yes, my dear, he is still here,' he said.

'Then he does not know,' she moaned, and closed her eyes.

The Doctor's position was an embarrassing

one. He was not in his patient's confidence, nor, indeed, after that first visit of his, had he been in that of her sisters. Mr. Roscoe was like a book clasped and locked to him, or, as he himself expressed it, like a railway company of whose time-table 'Bradshaw' scornfully remarks, 'No information.'

With Walter Sinclair, however, the Doctor had had some talk, and was thoroughly acquainted with that young gentleman's sentiments, as well as with his views of the situation.

'It doesn't much signify, my dear, what he knows, or what he does not know,' answered the Doctor dryly; 'he cares for nothing except to hear about you. If he has any regard for me, it is as for one of his old Indian friends, and Mr. Richard's, because I am the "Medicine Man," and in attendance upon you. Every morning it is "How is Grace?" and never "How do *you* do?"'

Her eyes were lit up for a moment with

an intense delight, which slowly died away as she replied with a sigh :

'I can't see him—I *daren't* see him.'

'Of course not, my dear. The thing is not to be dreamt of at present—or perhaps, as you were about to say, even at all. Still he will remain here till you are well and strong. Now tell me, is there anything you can think of that will give you pleasure?'

'Nothing, *nothing*!' she moaned despairingly.

'A friend of yours has been writing almost every day to me, one who loves you very much in a fatherly sort of way; when you get a little stronger, don't you think you would like to see *him*?'

'Yes. I should like to see Mr. Allerton very much.'

Dr. Gardner nodded, and put no more questions. He was more than satisfied with the state of his patient. He had the reputation of leaving those he attended upon too soon upon the road to recovery, not so much because he shrank from the least imputation of making the most of them as from his horror of humbug; but Grace Tremenhere's case was an exceptional one in his eyes. He knew that he should soon see her convalescent in its ordinary sense, but he wanted to see her cured, which would, he felt, be a very different thing. So interested had he been in the matter that he had taken the unusual step of communicating with Mr. Allerton, by whom his good intentions had been thoroughly appreciated. It is possible for two honest men to understand one another, even upon paper; and it would have amazed the Council of the Law Association to know how many letters—and those long ones—one of its most eminent members had written without charging his correspondent sixpence for them. He had readily promised that in case of Grace's recovery he would come down to Halswater and see her, though he detested the country in winter, and long journeys—unless at so much per foot—at all times.

Grace was not, however, of course, in a condition to bear such an interview, and in the meanwhile Dr. Gardner discouraged the presence of her sisters about his patient as much as possible. He saw that she shrank from them, though he could not guess the cause; which was no slur on his sagacity, for she could hardly have explained it herself. What troubled her almost as much as her estrangement from her lover was the new and terrible light which Mr. Roscoe had thrown upon her father's character; and though she had accepted it to a certain extent, she was, strangely enough, more apprehensive now than she had been before of hearing anything from their lips to his disadvantage. She need not have been so, for they had both something else to think about much more pressing than their father's memory, but from Mr. Allerton she felt she would get the truth, without the alloy of disappointment or resentment. She had little hope but that Mr. Roscoe's account of the manner in which Walter's father had been tricked and ruined was correct; the more her mind dwelt upon it—and it shared her mind with that other wretchedness which was its consequence—the more she felt that he could not have invented a story so capable of refutation, but still he might have exaggerated it for his own purposes. If it was true, in its disgraceful entirety, would Walter be still staying on under the same roof with her? She was obliged, alas! to answer for him— because she knew he loved her so—that that might be the case. For her sake he would forgive all, perhaps, and be content to wed with shame, for it was with her father's shame that she identified herself; and it rested with her to prevent the sacrifice.

To the mind, not only of the man of the world, but of any person of average common sense who has over-lived those social superstitions, which are to the full as monstrous as our spiritual ones, this sensitiveness of feeling may seem ridiculous. If one has done nothing wrong oneself, how can one be smirched by another's wrong? But even otherwise honest and good men are found to be so cruel and unjust as to think ill of a person because of his illegitimacy, and Grace was no more illogical than they—indeed, had her case been another's she would have taken a just view of it, but to some sensitive and delicate natures injustice loses its wrong when they are themselves its victims.

In those days of growing convalescence there was at least one comfort to Grace, that Mr. Roscoe did not come near her. She dreaded beyond everything to see the man that had destroyed the edifice both of her faith and of her love, and she wondered at her immunity from this infliction. Agnes wondered also; it seemed so strange that Edward, who always did exactly what was right, should not have seized the first opportunity to congratulate the girl upon her recovery, but she did not make any observation to him on the matter; the relations between them had become strained on account of her refusal to assist him with a loan of larger amount than usual. She was not fond of lending her money even to him, and perhaps she reflected that his finding himself short of it would hasten his movements in the direction which she still wished him to take as much as ever. She was tired of waiting for this laggard lover, and at the same time resented his making use of her property without having established the right to do so. Moreover his application had been couched in much less loving and seductive tones than he had hitherto given himself the trouble to use. He was getting impatient and reckless. Philippa, on the other hand, was not surprised that he was loth to intrude himself upon the presence of one whom his revelations had made so miserable; but that was not in fact the cause of Mr. Roscoe's failure in what Agnes termed 'a natural attention.' His position had become too perilous, his temper was too severely tried, to admit of his conforming even to the most ordinary conventions. If either sister had remonstrated with him for his neglect of their invalid he would probably have said that he did not care one farthing whether she was dead or alive.

Neither of them did so, though for very different reasons, and what affected Agnes much more than his brutal indifference to Grace was his growing familiarity with Philippa. This had become very marked; for though his behaviour towards her was in no respect more tender than it had been, he was constantly in her company and alone. They walked together in the garden and in particular on the cliff terrace above the lake, at the end of which a tower, or 'Folly,' as it was called by the neighbours, had been erected. It was scarcely used even in warm weather, though it had been designed as a summer-house, and it was strange indeed that it should have attractions for anybody at the present time when the mountains were covered with snow and the waters sealed by frost. No one but a woman who has felt jealousy could understand the rage that filled the heart of Agnes Tremenhere when she first saw her sister and Edward Roscoe leave the garden and climb the steps that led to the cliff terrace together. It was not love that took him there, but only the desire of speaking with his companion—on a very different subject—without fear of interruption; but Agnes thought it was love, or rather the pretence of it, which was almost as bad. And Philippa knew that she thought it, and was not displeased.. She had often made her sister jealous, but never with such apparently good reason, for Edward's caution had hitherto restrained her; but now he did not seem to care for prudence. Philippa thus took her revenge in feminine fashion for many a snub and slight she had received at her sister's hands.

One afternoon Agnes was in the sick room paying a more perfunctory visit to 'her dear Grace' even than usual; there was no longer any cause for anxiety on the patient's account, and her thoughts were just now dwelling upon other things—the fact that Roscoe and Philippa were walking together in the garden below for one thing. She was not even talking with Grace, upon whom at the moment the nurse was attending, but idly engaged herself in turning over the leaves of a school history she had taken down from its shelf. It had been one of Grace's lesson-books, not so long ago, when Philippa had been her governess, and was divided into portions with a note here and there in Philippa's hand. On some occasion when she had taken up that book, it is probable that her mind, like that of Agnes at the present moment, was astray from the subject before her, and had dwelt on other things. One historic passage had the phrase 'Philippa, Edward's queen' in it, and the blue pencil in some wandering moment had underscored the words. The writer had doubtless merely wished to see 'how it looked,' with the intention of rubbing it out again, but she had forgotten to do so, and there it stood, 'Philippa, Edward's queen,' *in italics.* The writing on the wall of Belshazzar's palace could scarcely have filled those who saw it with deeper emotion than that which the sight of that blue line evoked in their reader, but the meaning in her case had nothing of mystery in it; it was its very plainness that drove the colour from her cheek and turned her heart to stone. How shameful was it that Philippa had dared to indulge in a day-dream such as this! She tore out the leaf and placed it in her bosom

—a proof indeed of the treachery she had long suspected. As she did so, her eyes chanced to glance at the window, and through it perceived her sister and her companion ascending the winding steps that led to the terrace. With a wild cry which startled Grace in her pillowed chair she rushed from the room.

CHAPTER XLVI

'SHE IS MY WIFE'

THE shades of early evening were already falling, and the day had been bitterly cold, but Agnes Tremenhere delayed only long enough to throw on her bonnet and shawl before taking her way to the terrace. There was a fire in her blood that prevented her from feeling the fog that was rising from the mere, or the wintry air upon the hill-top. We cannot hold a fire in our hand by thinking of the frosty Caucasus, but passion is stronger than imagination, and can for a time ignore all physical inconveniences; she trembled in every limb, but it was not with cold. As she hurried up the winding steps that led to the cliff-top she had no definite purpose in view, she had not thought of what to say or what to do; a blind instinct of rage and hate impelled her to seek out the treacherous pair, and tax one of them at least with her perfidy. The proof of it, that lay in her bosom and seemed to burn it, was slight indeed; but coming as it did upon the top of a hundred corroborating circumstances, and, above all, at a moment when her jealousy was at its height, it brought conviction with it. Philippa, 'Edward's queen.' She tried to think of the shameless woman only, and not of her companion; she could not bear to picture *him* as yielding to temptation. It was impossible that for all these years he could have paid court to her, given her, tacitly but unmistakably, to understand that his life was bound up in hers, and of late that nothing but mere pecuniary details prevented their becoming one in the eyes of all as they had long been in their inmost hearts, and yet have been deceiving her. These are things common enough with lovers, but of which no woman believes her lover capable. Her rival in his affection is, on the other hand, capable of anything. She will tell Philippa what she thinks of her, and in Edward's presence, so that hereafter he shall have no excuse for being deceived.

Those she is in search of are not on the terrace, but in the 'Folly,' a roomy and solid structure, with a stone chamber below, intended to be used as a kitchen for the accommodation of picnic parties, and above, a well-lighted apartment commanding an extensive view. The windows are of particoloured glass, through which the landscape is supposed to be seen under the aspects of the four seasons. Unlike the seasons of the soul, wherein it is more difficult to recall our hours of adversity when we are happy than to picture our happiness when we are miserable, it is an easier task to portray winter in summer than summer in winter. There is no pane, however brightly hued, that can then bring back the hour 'of splendour in the grass, of glory in the flower.' At this time of year, even at noonday, the room with its spare summer furniture looks bare and melancholy, in unison with the fog and frost without. Its tenants, too, are wretched-looking; they are standing by one of the windows, and fix their gaze upon it, not because the wintry scene has any attraction for them, but because each prefers it to looking into the other's face. They have not exactly quarrelled, but they have disagreed, and are very dissatisfied, though not in the same degree, with one another. It is not without difficulty that Roscoe can conceal his exasperation against his companion for her obstinacy in refusing his request for a sum of money which he has told her is necessary for the re-establishment of his fortunes. It is necessary, indeed, for him to obtain it, though not for that purpose; it is wanted to stave off impending ruin, but that he dares not tell her. He can only use the same arguments he has often used before on less pressing occasions.

'Five thousand pounds is such a monstrous sum,' she pleads. 'To give you money is like pouring water into a sieve. Not that I grudge you, Edward. Hush, what's that?'

The door at the top of the short flight of stairs is open, but they have no fear of interruption, and do not sink their voices as they speak. Mr. Roscoe, indeed, speaks loudly and vehemently, his habits of caution, great and small, having alike disappeared in these later days. He pays no attention to his companion's interpolated inquiry, but answers scornfully:

'Grudge me? I hope not indeed. I think I have some claim upon you, Philippa.'

'You have indeed, dear Edward, every claim, but——'

'What claim?' cries a terrible voice, at which Philippa shrieks aloud, and even Roscoe for a moment trembles.

Agnes is standing in the doorway, her flaming eyes fixed upon her sister, her hand pointing to her companion. 'What claim can you have on Edward Roscoe? Your treacherous and lying tongue is silent. Edward, I appeal to *you*.'

There was a moment of painful and embarrassed silence, and then the man doggedly replied: 'She is my wife.'

'Your wife! Philippa your wife? Then if you are not a liar you are a thief. You have been drawing her money—*my* money—under false pretences. Five thousand pounds! why that is half her fortune! Mr. Allerton shall know of this. So you are a rogue and a fool in one.'

'He is neither the one nor the other,' exclaimed Philippa. 'You would have never called him so had he married you instead of me.'

'You viper!'

'You offcast!'

'Hush, hush!' interrupted Roscoe imperiously. 'Go home, Philippa, and leave me to deal with her.'

'Home! She will have no home after to-morrow,' cried Agnes furiously. 'You have wasted her miserable fortune for her before you began to steal what is mine by rights. And as for you who have beggared her, you will go to gaol.'

Her injurious words, spoken too in another's presence, would at any time have chafed Edward Roscoe's spirit beyond endurance, but now, in that moment of despair, with the consciousness that his long-cherished plans were futile and their object known, his face was like that of a baffled tiger.

'Go *home*, Philippa,' he repeated, with angry vehemence.

'One would think you were speaking to a dog,' said Agnes, with a grating laugh; 'and like a dog she sneaks away. I am glad to see it.'

Philippa's exit, indeed, was far from dignified. Notwithstanding her last brave words she was frightened at her sister, and reassured only by the knowledge that she had her husband to back her. Now that he had ordered her away, her turkey-like exhibition of wrath was over; she felt like a boned turkey. She tottered downstairs, and hurried along the bleak terrace, where the evening fog was thickening, towards the house. Its lights were already lit, and offered for the present at least a welcome. Was it really true, as Agnes had told her, that she had no longer a right to share its shelter? It was quite true that she had already given to Edward the whole sum, and more, that she had inherited under her father's will, in case she should marry in defiance of its restrictions. Had he indeed brought himself within the grasp of the law? That Agnes would show them no mercy she was well convinced. And did she deserve mercy? Had she not by her own misconduct hurried her father, though undesignedly, to his death? The thought had often occurred to her, and always with a remorseful shock, but never with greater force than now. When she reached the house, fortunately unseen by anyone, and locked the door of her own room behind her, that did not shut out this reflection. She threw herself into a chair, and covered her eyes with her hands, but the awful scene presented itself to her with greater distinctness than ever. It was the night of the conflagration at the theatre. Grace had come home in safety, and her father had not been aroused. The least shock the doctor had said might prove fatal, but the news of her peril had been spared to him, and she rejoiced at it, though she was well aware that her husband was calculating on the old man's death. Edward and she had been married many months, and were only waiting for it to announce the fact. The terms of his will were unknown to them.

. It was very late, and Edward was bidding her good night in the corridor. She had been dreadfully upset by the events of the evening, and his manner was unusually tender and comforting; he had his arm round her waist, and was giving her a farewell kiss, when a door was suddenly opened, and her father stood before them in his dressing-gown.

'What is this?' he cried, addressing his confidential assistant. 'How dare you? And you, you shameless slut?'

'Father dear, he is my husband,' pleaded Philippa.

Those were the last words that passed between them. Poor 'Josh' fell forward on his face and never spoke again. They carried him back into his room, but even if they had dared to send for help it would have availed him nothing. In a few minutes he was a dead man. It was no wonder that Mr.

Allerton had found Philippa the next day agitated by such unexpected emotion. Though she had got over the dreadful experience in time, and, as we have seen, could even join with Agnes in her denunciations of her father's memory, she never forgot that it was her own conduct which had cut short his life. It was a string that Mr. Roscoe had often played upon, and it had always vibrated to his touch. Sometimes she even said to herself, 'I am a murderess.' At others, when it was her husband's *rôle* to make light of her part in the matter, she took it less to heart; but just now remorse was gripping her. Oh! why did Edward not come? Why did he leave her alone with these awful thoughts? What could he have to say to Agnes that had so long delayed him? At last there was a knock at the door she knew, for they had many such secret signs, these two; and Edward stood before her, pale, wild-looking, and breathless.

'What did Agnes say? What do you think she will do?' she inquired anxiously. 'Have you made it up in any way?'

'Yes,' he answered in a hollow voice. 'I think she is somewhat pacified.' He sank into a chair, and wiped his forehead with his handkerchief. 'Have you any brandy? No, don't go down for it,' he put in sharply, for she was moving quickly towards the door. She pitied his condition, which, indeed, was easily to be accounted for. What an interview must he have had, poor fellow, and all through his own boldness in confessing that he was married to her! Notwithstanding its probable consequences she admired him for that. It was a declaration which she had long desired to make herself, at all hazards.

'Agnes keeps a little brandy in her room, but perhaps she came home with you, and I dare not meet her.'

'She did not come back,' he answered, 'but the brandy is no matter. Stay where you are. Let us be together,' and he looked round him apprehensively.

'Dear Edward, that is what we shall now always be,' she replied caressingly. 'Out of this seeming harm, as you have often told me, good may, perhaps will, come to us. For my part I am sick of our long career of secrecy and deception. Money is not everything after all.'

She rather expected an outburst from him against her 'sentimental folly,' but there was none. His face showed no trace of anger, but wore a listening air, as though he was willing to hear her speak on. He even suffered her to take his hand and fondle it.

'There may be trouble before us, Edward, but it cannot be so hard to bear, so far as I am concerned, as what I have suffered of late. To live under the same roof with Agnes was getting insupportable ; and, even if you had not spoken out as you did just now, it could not have lasted much longer. However she may behave to us, dear Grace will, I know, be our friend, though I fear we have not deserved it. Is it not possible, now that things have happened as they have done, that we may do her a good turn?'

What she felt, but did not say, was, 'Now that your own plan has miscarried, there can be no reason for making her unhappy, and I think you could make matters straight between her and Walter if you chose.' She had still great faith in his cleverness, though, alas, but little in his sense of right.

He nodded, as she hoped in approval, and she went on with rising spirits:

'Mr. Allerton, though he is no friend of yours, is devoted to Grace, and has some influence with even Agnes; I am sure that he will effect some kind of settlement. It would be quite contrary to his wish that there should be any public disruption of the family. We must leave Halswater, of course, but it need not be under a cloud.'

'Yes, Allerton is the man,' he murmured, with a sigh of relief; 'he will patch things up for Grace's sake. What's that?' he cried, suddenly springing to his feet. 'Why are they tolling the church bell?'

'My dear Edward, what is the matter with you?' she exclaimed apprehensively. 'That is not the church bell; it is the gong for afternoon tea.'

'To be sure, I had forgotten,' he answered moodily, and sat down again.

'But what am I to do, Edward? I daren't go down alone to meet her. You *must* come down with me. Do you think it possible that she will break out again before Walter and your brother?'

'No.'

'Then I will go down and pour out the tea as usual. It will be best to treat her, for the present, even if we go to-morrow, as if nothing had happened.'

He did not answer her, though he still

wore that listening look. The beating of the gong had ceased, but the wind was rising, and howled without like some unhappy disembodied spirit.

'Did anyone see you return to the house, Philippa?' he suddenly inquired with great earnestness.

'No one.'

'Nor me. That is so far fortunate. Now listen; we two came in together, leaving Agnes on the terrace.'

'But we didn't, Edward.'

'Hush, you fool! I say we *did*. She said she wanted a bracing walk, and we left her there, pacing up and down. There was no quarrel between us of any kind. Do you understand?'

She did not understand, but she began to suspect. She stared at him with horrified eyes; her tongue clove to the roof of her mouth.

'You can keep a secret, I know,' he went

on in a menacing tone. ' You have kept more than one of your own. Keep mine.'

' Great heaven, what have you done ? ' she cried.

' Nothing. I left her there—*we* left her there; there is no parapet—she may have fallen over, into the lake for all I know. Come down to tea. There is no fear of meeting Agnes. Come.' He offered his hand, but she drew back, and kept him at arm's length. Her face expressed horror and disgust, nay, even hate.

' You don't feel well enough—a severe headache? Very well, I'll say so. Do as you please. Only remember we two came in together.' He was gone.

CHAPTER XLVII

ON THE SPOT

WHEN Mr. Roscoe went downstairs he found both his brother and Walter Sinclair in the drawing-room. They were neither of them much devoted to the institution of five o'clock tea, but they were generally present at it, because from one or other of the two sisters they learnt news from the sick room. The absence of both Agnes and Philippa on the present occasion made them not a little anxious.

'Have you any news?' inquired Walter of Mr. Roscoe.

'No,' he answered; 'she has not come in yet.' The instant the words had passed his lips he owned his folly. Was he becoming an idiot because of what had happened, that he could not get it out of his thoughts for an instant, and must imagine that everybody else was equally occupied with the subject? 'I thought you were referring to the absence of Miss Agnes,' he continued carelessly, in reply to the others' look of amazement. 'She is still out of doors; and unfortunately Miss Philippa, I am informed, has one of her bad headaches, and will not be here to do the honours of the tea-table, so we must help ourselves.'

As they did not seem inclined to do this, Mr. Roscoe poured out the tea for them, but not with his usual neatness of hand; he was thinking of something else—listening again—and spilt it. Walter noticed his preoccupation, and guessed its cause—or a part of it.

'Miss Agnes cannot surely be out of doors in this weather; it is snowing.'

'Thank heaven!' exclaimed Mr. Roscoe mechanically.

We often do thank heaven for strange things, even for things that would appear to have their origin in quite another place; just as we often, alas! pray to heaven for gifts that are far from celestial in their nature, and which can only be secured at the expense of our fellow-creatures. Still the strangeness of Mr. Roscoe's exclamation attracted the attention of both his hearers.

'What on earth should you want snow for?' inquired his brother.

Richard's manner, like his own, had undergone some change of late. He had never been so subservient to Edward as it was his obvious duty (or at all events his interest) to be; but he had now become irritable and antagonistic. He took little pains to conceal the opinion he entertained of his nature and projects. Edward had come to the conclusion that it would be necessary to get rid of this relative, who had the insolence to ban what he had been sent for to bless, and so far from being a helpmate was a hinder-mate ; only just now much more serious matters than his dismissal were on his mind.

'Well, you don't understand agricultural matters in England, my good fellow,' he answered, 'but the country wants snow. When that has fallen the frosts will probably break up.'

'At present, though the snow *is* falling,' replied Richard curtly, 'it is colder than ever.'

'It is strange indeed that in such inclement weather Miss Agnes should still be out of doors,' observed Walter, going to the window and throwing back its gilded shutter. 'The lights in the garden are lit, so that she must know it's late ; where has she gone?'

'Miss Philippa and I left her walking on the terrace,' said Mr. Roscoe, speaking with great distinctness. 'I told her it was near tea-time, but she said she felt in need of exercise, having been in attendance on her sister this afternoon, and would take a turn or two more.'

'The steps are very slippery this weather,' observed Walter; 'I think some one should go and look after her.'

There was no reply to this remark, so Walter left the room, put on his great-coat, and went out. It was already dark, and the snow was falling heavily, so that it was not easy, even by help of the garden lamps, to find one's way to the winding steps that led to the terrace, though Walter had keen eyes, which had been used to heavier snows than ever fall in Westmoreland. It was certainly no evening for a delicate woman to be abroad in. He thought it possible that Miss Agnes might be snow-bound or fog-bound in the summer-house, and afraid to venture back along the unprotected walk, with its cliff descending down into the lake, so for the summer-house he made. Its door was standing open, which corroborated his view of the

matter, and he went upstairs crying 'Miss
Agnes, Miss Agnes!' in order not to alarm
her by his sudden entrance. It was an unnecessary precaution. The room which had
of late been the scene of such a stormy interview was empty, and in place of those voices
of passion there was only the shrill cry of the
wind, and the soft crush of the snow as it
huddled against the window-pane. 'Miss
Agnes, Miss Agnes!' Heaven only knows
whether she heard him, but there was no
response. Walter was now seriously alarmed.
It was next to impossible that she could have
wandered off the terrace on the landward
side, because she would have had the lights
from the Hall to guide her, but it *was* possible
that in keeping too near them she had fallen
over the cliff. On his way back he met both
the Roscoes with servants and lanterns, and
they made what search they could, but the
whirling snow hid everything. Before that
began to fall the marks of the passage of any

heavy body down the friable steep would have been discernible, but it was now hopeless to detect them. The lake beneath had become unapproachable, for while no boat could be put on it on account of its icy covering, the ice was not thick enough—it seldom was in 'fathomless Halswater'—to bear the weight of a human being. There was nothing for it but to wait for the morning, and in the meantime to hope. It was just possible that even now Agnes had reached home by some other route.

It was a terrible night for the whole household—sickening to those who suffered from suspense, and far worse to those who knew. Agnes was not popular, but as they thought of her, lost in the whirling snow or drowned in the frozen lake, it was not her defects that were dwelt upon. She had been a hard woman, but not an unjust one; prudent, but not close-fisted; a good but not over-exacting housekeeper. If this is not

much to say in her favour, and yet all hearts
(save one) bled for her for pity's sake, think
what suspense must mean to households (there
are thousands of them) whose breadwinner is
at sea, 'given up' at Lloyd's, but not at home,
or whose darling is reported 'missing' in the
wars! Heaven shield us, reader, from such
miseries. A score of times the doors were
opened to the night, and anxious faces peered
into the white gloom; a score of times there
was heard, or seemed to be heard, a knocking,
a tap, a voice, and they said 'Hush!' or 'That
is she!' But she came not. Grace, of course,
knew nothing of her absence; she had sor-
rows of her own enough, and was spared that
awful watch. But Philippa—Philippa was
more to be pitied than even Agnes. She
knew, though she tried to persuade herself
that she knew not; or at all events she knew
that her husband knew. With that knowledge all love for him—the last relics of it—
had fled from her bosom; nay, the very fact

that it had ever filled it increased her loathing for the man. The recollection even of her own antagonism to Agnes increased it. In cutting short her sister's life he had deprived herself (oh cruel and remorseless wretch!) of the hope of reconcilement.

'I did not kill her,' Roscoe said to his wife that night, 'so help me heaven! It was her own fault. As we were walking home together she stepped backward and fell over the cliff.'

Philippa answered nothing, but her face said, 'You lie.'

He felt that all was over between them as regarded affection—as, indeed, it had long been on his side; one foe the more, one would have thought, could not have made much difference. He was now an outcast from his kind, without one single tie to them save that of self-interest. We know what comes of the 'solitary system' in gaol, *at first*—how the heart of the prisoner is filled with hatred and malice against the whole world, which he accuses of having devised, or permitted, his punishment. Something of this feeling took possession of Edward Roscoe. He would revenge himself on humanity—or at all events on all those to whom he owed a grudge, or who were obnoxious to him—on the first opportunity; but in the meantime there was a more pressing matter to be attended to, his own personal safety. Though Philippa was not to be trusted, in any gracious sense of the word, he felt he could rely on her, whatever might be her suspicions, not to denounce him. If she had resolved not to assist him with that statement of their having come home together from the terrace, she would have said so. He saw that she was no longer afraid of him, that hate had cast out fear, but that her silence in this connection meant consent. Even if she did witness against him, her evidence would be valueless in law, for was she not his wife? But that was a revelation, unless pushed to it very hard, he would certainly not make at such a juncture.

Throughout that night to no inmate of the Hall, save the invalid girl, came balmy sleep. Anxiety for Agnes, or at least a wild excitement, agitated every bosom. At last on the blank scene rose the blank day; the snow shroud was over all things, and the snow still falling with silent persistence. There was no trace of the lost woman to be seen anywhere, but all the probabilities pointed to one direction. The narrow dangerous footway that could just be followed in summer, on the margin of the steep side of Halswater, was of course invisible, and the only means of approach to the lake was by letting down men by ropes from the terrace, who at great risk of immersion swept the snow away from its ice-bound surface.

At last was found, not indeed what they sought, for that was impossible, but a spot where the ice was very thin, and round it signs of fracture. Some heavy body had evidently fallen through with great force on the previous evening, and though the night's frost had sealed up the hole, and the snow in its turn had covered it, the fate that had befallen Agnes Tremenhere was sufficiently revealed. Any attempt to rescue the body was for the present useless; there it lay 'full fathom five,' and deeper yet, and must needs lie until the ice melted and the water could be dragged. It was no wonder that Edward Roscoe had said 'Thank heaven!' when he had heard that the snow was falling, for it concealed all evidence, if evidence there was, of what had happened on land, while the lake could be trusted to keep its own secret. There could be no inquest, so he had nothing to fear from Philippa's weakness; he told his own story, and, as he had calculated, she did not gainsay it.

They had left her sister walking by herself upon the terrace, in her usual health and spirits, and there was no reason for doubt how, in that dangerous spot, she had come by her end.

To everyone else, however, these circumstances greatly added to the horror of the catastrophe. It is no matter to ourselves, when our spirit has fled, what becomes of its poor human tenement, but to those belonging to us it makes a difference. It is far worse to us, 'the fools of habit,' as the poet tells us, that 'hands so often clasped in ours should toss with tangle and shell'—that the 'vast and wandering grave' of ocean should environ one familiar to us—than that he should lie 'neath the churchyard sod. In Agnes's case, so near her home and yet so far from it, the circumstances were even more painful, yet not even Philippa thought of leaving the Hall; it seemed to be an act of desertion towards one whom she had already wronged enough. She would wait there until the last rites could be paid to her sister.

Nor did Edward attempt to dissuade her. One would have thought he would have been eager to leave a scene which, whatever part he had played in it, must have been at least an awful one to look back upon. On the contrary, he often sought the terrace alone, though never after nightfall. It is possible that with some return of his old caution he did so to make assurance sure that there was nothing left there of a compromising character, or perhaps there was some morbid attraction for him in the place such as is said to coerce those who have the guilt of blood upon their souls to revisit the scene of their crime. But in my opinion it was the former reason. Just as a good man will entertain no scruple about having killed some cruel wretch in the act of attempting the murder of some innocent girl, so it is probable Edward Roscoe experienced no remorse in the contemplation of the fate of one who had always been as a millstone about his neck, and whose last act had been to denounce and threaten him with punishment. My belief is that after the first few hours of terror and excitement, when he was certainly far from being himself, he thought of it no more (except for its possible consequences) than a chess-player who sweeps a piece from his adversary's board. What had happened, though there was doubtless danger in it, was so far of great advantage to him. To a certain extent it even strengthened his hands, not only by its leaving fewer adversaries to deal with, but by increasing that courage of despair which he had of late experienced. He felt that his masterful nature would now stick at nothing, and drew from it the conclusion that nothing—in the way of defeat—could stop him. Indeed, he had already reaped some material benefit. Though his wife showed the utmost loathing for him when they chanced to be alone together, and would even remain stubbornly silent when he addressed her upon any subject in connection with her lost sister, he found her unexpectedly subservient in pecuniary matters. She signed certain documents—the very ones she had hitherto refused to sign—which enabled him to tide over his more pressing difficulties. 'What is money to me *now*?' she said in despairing tones. 'Take what you will of it, since you have taken all besides'—a state of mind which, in a wife with a large banking account of her own, seemed to him laudable and meritorious in the highest degree.

Mr. Allerton, however, whose visit to Halswater this catastrophe to its mistress had naturally precipitated, was coming to the Hall at once, a circumstance that was by no means so welcome. There was nothing to discover, of course, but there were persons under that roof, Mr. Roscoe knew, who regarded him with unfavourable eyes, and he did not wish their wits to be sharpened by contact with those of the family lawyer.

CHAPTER XLVIII

A COMFORTER

When Mr. Allerton arrived at Halswater he was pleasurably disappointed, as our English 'bull' runs, in not being made welcome, as usual, by the *de facto* master of the house. It had hitherto been Mr. Edward Roscoe's custom to receive all guests that visited the Tremenhere ladies as if they had been his own, but on the present occasion he did not even give himself the trouble to depute that office. So it strangely enough happened that Mr. Allerton was received by Walter Sinclair—a person who, so far from having any authority to welcome him to the Hall, had himself, as we know, but a precarious footing there. Moreover the last letter in which the lawyer had mentioned his name had been by no means a letter of recommendation; it had been that which he had written to Grace, remonstrating with her on the encouragement she had given to the young man, and pointing out how very undesirable from a practical point of view he would be as a husband, and Walter knew that he had written it. So fair and honest was the young man's character, however, that he felt no spark of resentment against the lawyer on that account—he was Grace's guardian, he reflected, and simply doing his duty—but only remembered the kindnesses he had personally received at the other's hands.

'I am so glad you are come, Mr. Allerton,' he exclaimed as they shook hands warmly; 'things are all going on here as in a ship without a rudder.'

He took him to his room, which was in 'the Cottage,' next his own, and the two had a long talk together, but without touching on the subject which had placed them in antagonism to one another.

'First, about poor Miss Agnes?' said the lawyer. 'Tell me frankly, what is your view?'

Walter raised his eyes in some astonishment.

'There is nothing to tell but what has been told you. Mr. Roscoe and Miss Philippa left her on the terrace. It is a dangerous spot except in the daytime for anybody, as you will see for yourself. It was evening, and snowing heavily; there is not a doubt that the poor lady fell into the lake.'

'A ghastly catastrophe, indeed,' observed the other gravely. 'And of course Miss Grace knows nothing about it?'

'Nothing. It would be madness to tell her. Dr. Gardner will give you an account of her condition; he comes here this afternoon instead of the morning on purpose to do so. We have every confidence in him.'

'Whom do you mean by "we"?'

Walter flushed up to his eyes. 'It was an expression I own I had no right to use,' he said apologetically. 'I am quite aware that I have no recognised position here, but everything, as I have hinted, is topsyturvy.'

'It was always that,' observed the lawyer dryly; 'or at least the person who had the least right to be there was at the head of affairs. He is so still, I suppose, and more than ever.'

'In a sort of way, yes; but, on the other hand, he does not take so much upon himself; he seems to care little how things go.'

'What has happened—as indeed it well may do—monopolises his thoughts, I conclude?'

The lawyer's words were indifferent, but not his tone. He seemed to be awaiting some reply from his companion and with anxiety, though there hardly seemed occasion for a reply.

'No doubt; this terrible event has unhinged us all, and brought us into new relations. That is why I used the word "we" just now, for Miss Philippa takes me a good deal into her confidence.'

'And not Mr. Roscoe?' inquired the lawyer sharply.

'I can't say about that, but she certainly seems to avoid his society, which, as you know, she did not use to do. There are many changes here,' replied the young fellow.

'I suppose so; that was to be expected. There is one change for the better, however, I am glad to find from Dr. Gardner's letters. Have you seen Grace?'

'I? Certainly not, sir. She has forbidden me—that is, before she was taken ill, and as I was given to understand in consequence of some communication from yourself, she forbad me to see her.'

'Indeed. Who told you that?'

'She told me herself—that is, in her own handwriting.'

'Let me see it.'

Walter went into his own room and produced the slip of paper she had written to him: 'Seek,' &c.

The lawyer examined the manuscript very carefully.

'Mr. Roscoe brought you that communication?' he remarked.

'Yes. But it is Grace's handwriting,' replied Walter in response to an expression on the other's face. 'Miss Philippa corroborates the fact—so far. Still the affair is unintelligible to me, in some respects—though perhaps not to you?' he added with a touch of bitterness.

To this question the lawyer made no rejoinder; he shifted his chair and gazed absently before him, evidently in deep thought.

'What sort of a person is this Mr. Richard Roscoe?' he inquired presently.

'A very honest fellow, but eccentric. He has had troubles—perhaps has them now—which I sometimes fear have affected his mind.'

'Is he on good terms with his brother?'

'There is no open quarrel between them, but there is certainly no love lost. He mistrusts Mr. Edward very much, I think.'

'He must be mad indeed if he didn't,' was Mr. Allerton's cynical reply. 'If that man was an American he would be called "the Champion Scoundrel." Does he see much of Grace?'

'He has never seen her, I understand, since the interview in which she gave him that writing. So at least Miss Philippa tells me.'

'Who does see her?'

'Only Miss Philippa, the Doctor, and the nurse—— Here *is* the Doctor.'

Dr. Gardner in his high boots and with his riding whip in hand was at 'the Cottage' door. Walter introduced the two men to one another, and left them together. When they came out after a protracted talk they had both very serious faces.

'I will just look to my patient, Mr.

Allerton, and if she is well enough she shall then see *you*.'

The lawyer nodded: a complete understanding seemed to have been arrived at by these two men.

In due course Mr. Allerton was summoned to the sick room. Grace was sitting up in her chair, but still too weak to rise to welcome him. It was a sad meeting, and at first, to his great distress, she gave way to tears.

'That won't hurt her,' said the old Doctor with a wise brutality. 'She would have been better by now had there been more tears.'

He left the room, taking the nurse with him.

'I have been wanting to see you, dear Mr. Allerton, these many weeks,' said Grace, placing her thin hand on his. 'You are the only person in whom I have any trust.'

'I am sorry to hear you say that, my dear.'

'Yes; you are the only person I now see (except, indeed, the good Doctor, who cannot help me) in whom I have any confidence. Agnes never comes near me; Philippa is kind, but strangely altered in other respects. They are the only two persons who can answer the question I have to put to you, and I would not apply to them in any case. Mr. Allerton, tell me truly, what was dear papa?'

The lawyer had come down to Halswater prepared to hear strange things, and with stranger things in his own mind than he was likely to hear, but this inquiry was wholly unlooked for, and his face showed it. For the moment he was silent.

'Do not deceive me,' she said plaintively; 'let me know the whole truth.'

'Your father, my dear girl, as everybody knew except yourself, was a money-lender. It is not a calling that is thought highly of, but he was at the head of it; moreover, it does not follow that a money-lender——'

'Was he an honest man?' she interrupted vehemently.

'Yes. For a money-lender, as I have always said, exceptionally honest.'

'Money is the root of all evil,' observed Grace with a sigh and a shudder.

'It is so stated in the copy-books, my dear, and no doubt there is truth in it. It is bad to beg and bad to borrow, and the trade of lending it is not what one calls a liberal education; still there are money-lenders and money-lenders, and your father was the best specimen of his trade I have ever known.'

'Why did he hide it from me? Why did everybody hide it from me?' she murmured reproachfully.

'Well, for the very reasons I have mentioned. Your father was so passionately fond of you——'

'His little Fairy,' she interrupted, in a trembling voice. 'Heaven knows how I loved him!'

'And also how he loved you, my dear. He always wished you to think the best of him, as we all do. I never should have told you I was a lawyer if I could have helped it. It was weakness in him to conceal the fact, but it was love that made him weak. The same sentiment in a less degree actuated your sisters; they had a grudge against your father, and did not spare his memory so far as they were themselves concerned, but they never strove to disturb your faith in him, and that is to their credit. For my part, I cannot imagine how you could have been ignorant of his profession.'

'I knew he lent his friends money, of course, and not for nothing. But I thought he did them good, and not harm. I did not know that he was'—she sank her voice to a whisper—'a usurer.'

'Who told you he was a usurer? But I need not ask. There is only one man in the world who could have done it.'

'But was it *true*?'

Her pleading eyes looked straight into the lawyer's face. His heart melted within him, but his composure remained outwardly firm.

'You need not answer,' she said despairingly. 'I see it was so; now tell me this. Did gold so weigh with him that kith and kin, justice and compassion, were nothing compared with it? Was he such a slave to greed that he could cheat one of his own blood of all he had, and thrive upon his ruin?'

'No! A thousand times, no!' replied the lawyer confidently; 'it is a lie, whoever told you so. In the first place he had no kith or kin except yourselves; in the second, in my judgment he was incapable of such conduct.'

'Are you sure of this?'

Even while she spoke he remembered that her father had mentioned to him when making his will that he had some faraway cousin ; but the matter seemed to have no reference to the subject on hand, and he yearned to put that torn and tender heart at rest. 'I am quite sure,' he answered.

'In my father's papers, in which you told me every business transaction of his was noted down, was there any word of one with my—with Walter Sinclair's father? It was in connection with some mine in Cornwall.'

'Certainly not. The name would certainly have struck me had it been otherwise. You may set your mind quite at ease, my dear, upon that point.'

'Thank heaven!' she murmured fervently; 'you have brought me from death to life, dear Mr. Allerton;' and rising feebly from her chair she kissed him.

CHAPTER XLIX

MR. ROSCOE'S CONGRATULATIONS

IT is probable that Grace's guardian had come down to Halswater in no very exacting mood towards his ward and favourite. The letter he had had from the Doctor had no doubt gone far to convince him that her complete recovery would be dependent upon the course of true love, which had been so cruelly interrupted, running for the future smoothly; and though it was both his duty and his desire to preserve her fortune for her, he felt that her health and happiness were still more important things; moreover, the fact, now patent to him, that Mr. Roscoe had by foul means broken the bond between the young couple, no doubt inclined him to mend it, and, above all, Grace had kissed him. Of course it was foolish of him to allow that last little matter to influence his conduct, but as a matter of fact it did, and he would have been worse than a fool had it been otherwise. The remembrance of how the girl he loved as though she had been his own daughter, weak and ill, and the mere shadow of her former self, had tottered out of her chair to thank him for his good tidings with a kiss, compelled him to obey her wishes as though they had been a decree of the Court of Chancery. After all, he had saved a little money for her in spite of her large charities, and she would have the ten thousand pounds which Josh had left—though less in love than to make his testament secure—to any of his daughters that should go counter to the provisions of his will; and Walter had a little money of his own, and a profession to follow.

Upon the whole, therefore, one may say that Mr. Allerton, instead of being an opponent of the young couple, had accepted a

retainer (from himself) on the other side. He
did not grudge Philippa the good luck which
would now make her for life, and possibly for
ever, the inheritress of her father's colossal
fortune; it was better, at all events, than if
Agnes (because she had been less kind to
Grace) had been in her place, though if he
had known Philippa's secret his views might
have altered altogether. To have found himself outwitted by Mr. Roscoe and *that* man the
master of Josh's million would have been
intolerable to the lawyer. In the present
relations, however (so far as he understood
them), between Philippa and him, no such
result seemed possible; and he could so far
afford to treat his enemy with great politeness.
What puzzled him was why Mr. Roscoe had
endeavoured to stop Grace's marriage. So
long as he kept on good terms with the other
two sisters, as had until lately seemed to be
the case, there was every reason why he
should have encouraged it. The person over

whom he exercised so great an influence would have been far the richer by it; and indeed there had been a time when he had certainly wished Grace to marry. However, it was obvious, whatever his reason, that he did not wish it now, and therefore Mr. Allerton could not resist the temptation of telling him with his own lips that the young couple were in a fair way of being reconciled.

'There has been some unfortunate misunderstanding, it seems,' he said, ' upon the part of Miss Grace, but you will be happy to hear that it has now been cleared away.'

It was in the garden, where, just after he left Grace's room, he found Mr. Roscoe walking to and fro, that the lawyer made this innocent communication to him.

Mr. Roscoe gave him such a look as, if looks could wither, would have left him a skeleton, but answered indifferently enough, ' That is good news indeed.'

That he did not ask for any explanation

of such unexpected tidings was proof positive to the lawyer that he did not dare to do so. This he did not need, however, as a corroboration of his view of Mr. Edward Roscoe's character, which had long been formed; of late days it had taken a dark tinge indeed, and if the other could have peeped into the lawyer's mind he would have been startled at the picture of himself he would have found there.

'Is Miss Grace sufficiently well to receive visitors?' inquired Mr. Roscoe presently.

'That depends; she has just seen *me*,' observed Mr. Allerton.

'Oh, of course; you are her guardian and her friend—which last indeed,' he added hastily, 'we all are. But I suppose anything liable to evoke excitement is still forbidden her?'

'The Doctor tells me Sinclair may be permitted to see her for a few minutes.'

'Oh!' — only a monosyllable, but it

seemed to say 'things have gone so far on the way of reconcilement as *that*, have they?'

'She will not, however, be able to see anyone else to-day, I should say,' continued Mr Allerton significantly.

He would have forbidden him the sick-room altogether if he could have done so with reason.

'That seems judicious,' observed the other coldly. 'Perhaps to-morrow she may be strong enough to receive my poor congratulations.'

In the meantime Walter had been permitted an interview with Grace, which was positively to last but a few minutes. Under such circumstances they were sure not to waste it in mere explanations which could be entered upon at any time if it was worth while; moreover Walter had been warned against them by the Doctor. The great point was that they were in each other's arms again.

'Heaven is very good to me,' murmured Grace in his ear. Walter smiled a little deprecatingly, as though he would have said, 'So it ought to be, for are you not one of its own angels?'

'I never thought to see you again, Walter, my darling, my darling! Oh, what have I not suffered!'

'No matter, sweetheart, it is all over now; you have only to get well.'

'I *am* well,' she answered; which was not quite true, but very pretty. The Beautiful and the True are not always the same thing, notwithstanding what the poets tell us.

'How could you, *could* you, bid me go away from you?' he whispered, not reproachfully, but with the air of one who asks for information.

'You may well ask; I must have been mad to believe them.'

'*Them*? What was it they said against me?' inquired Walter.

'Nothing. Do you think I should have believed them if they had?' she answered indignantly.

'Of course not,' he said. It sounded like complacency, but he had suddenly remembered that this was a forbidden subject. 'As soon as you are strong enough you are to go south, to the seaside,' he added hastily.

'What! away from you?'

'How could that be possible, darling? Where thou goest I will go.' He was about to continue the quotation with 'My people shall be thy people,' but felt it far from apposite and checked himself—not, however, as it appeared, in time.

'Do my sisters know that you are with me?' she asked.

'Yes,' he said unhesitatingly; the subject of Agnes was not of course to be discussed, but on the other hand reticence itself might provoke suspicion. 'Philippa was most kind in her congratulations; I believe she is genuinely fond of you.'

'It is sad to have to make exceptions,' she answered with a sigh. 'I wish to be at peace with all the world. I suppose Agnes will come to see me presently.'

The Doctor had entered the room as she was speaking.

'Not to-day, Miss Grace,' he observed cheerfully; 'you have had visitors enough. This one, indeed, flattered himself that you would not wish to see another after him—like leaving a pleasant taste in the mouth, which one is averse to lose by taking anything afterwards.'

'The Doctor is professional, even in his metaphors,' said Grace with a pleasant smile.

'I like to see my patients impudent,' returned the kindly old fellow. 'It may, however, be the result of intoxication; I think you have had enough of this stimulant, my dear,' he added, looking towards Walter. 'His five minutes are up.'

The young man arose at once. Though he had said so little, he felt that there had been no loss of time. He was another man already, or rather two beings in one. His heart was filled with love and gratitude, and had no room for ignoble thoughts. He had even forgiven his enemies since all their plans had failed. In the library he found the brothers, apparently in far from amicable discourse. In reply to their inquiries after Grace, he gave them all particulars save those which concerned himself. He knew that Richard's sympathy was genuine, and he could not believe just then that even Mr. Roscoe could be indifferent to his news. Nor did that gentleman seem indifferent; he was quite interested, indeed, in some parts of the narrative, and put several questions.

'Did she really look as if she had "turned the corner"? Was she in good spirits? Was the nurse always in her room? That Doctor, who dispensed his own medicines, gave her plenty of them, no doubt.'

Walter stood up for the Doctor, of whom Grace had spoken very warmly, and thought there had been nothing to complain of in that respect. 'She took no medicines now,' he said, ' except a strong tonic—strychnine.'

'A very dangerous thing,' observed Mr. Roscoe.

'It doesn't lie about,' said Walter, 'but is kept in the medicine chest in Miss Agnes's room, and administered only by the Doctor himself. He is a very careful fellow.'

Mr. Roscoe was glad to hear it, glad to hear such a good report of the dear invalid, glad to find (from Mr. Allerton) that the cloud that had shadowed the young people's prospects of late had given way to sunshine.

It would have seemed, in short, strange to Walter that Mr. Roscoe, in his effusiveness, had not shaken hands with him, but that he reflected that his offering to do so would have seemed too much like 'making up,' and it was evidently the other's endeavour to show that there was no need for that, nor ever had been. The young fellow was willing enough to find things on this footing. He was in Eden, and did not wish to be reminded of the existence of the serpent: he, too, wished to be at peace with everybody.

Curiously enough, Richard had manifested less concern in what he had to say than Edward, on whom he kept his eyes throughout with no very fraternal expression.

'I am afraid, Richard, you have been having some unpleasantness with your brother?' said Walter, when they found themselves alone together.

'Well, yes,' replied Richard reluctantly, 'we have each been telling the other what we thought of him.'

'That is bad,' answered Walter, though, in truth, nothing seemed bad, or at least unendurable, to him at that moment. 'It is like two women telling one another that they are ugly.'

'Well, we didn't say that,' replied Richard gravely, 'but let me tell you one thing: my brother is never so ugly as when he smiles, and he has been smiling on you. It is a bad sign.'

'Come, come, that is a jaundiced view indeed,' remonstrated Walter. 'Of course he is not pleased at the failure of his plans, though he pretends to be; but, like a gambler who has lost, he has made up his mind to pay up and look pleasant. Do not let us be hard upon him, when everything has turned out well. Oh, Richard, I am so happy.'

'You deserve to be,' sighed Richard. 'You are a good fellow. But do not let generosity to a fallen enemy carry you too far—to trust him, for instance. The Indian is never so dangerous as when he has received a mortal wound. I have seen a man kneel down by the side of one to give him a cup of water, and get a knife driven into his heart for his pains.'

CHAPTER L

HIS LAST THROW

GOOD news is the best of tonics, and the day after her interview with Walter, Grace felt that she had made great progress on the road to convalescence. The Doctor, who had hitherto come twice a day, was not to visit her in the afternoon, but in the morning, finding her both able and willing to receive visitors, he gave her permission to do so after the midday meal. He would have preferred such excitement to be postponed still a little longer, but his patient was nervously desirous to get both visits over—especially that of Mr. Roscoe, who had made tender application to see her. It was the less easy to refuse it since Agnes could not come, for a reason that they did not as yet dare tell her, but ascribed her absence to indisposition. If Grace felt equal to receiving two visitors she could certainly see one. In reality, she was neither so strong, nor so brave, as she represented herself to be. The last time she had seen Mr. Roscoe he had almost driven her into her grave with his falsehoods and insinuations; and though she had no fear of their being repeated, and was willing enough to let bygones be bygones, she could not forget them; but having once said 'I will see him,' she had not the courage to own herself a coward.

Philippa's tone, when she brought his message to her, had not been reassuring; she repeated it like a parrot, yet with an air of distress which to Grace was unaccountable.

'You must not be astonished,' she said, 'if you see some change in Mr. Roscoe. He has had his troubles like the rest of us.'

In the case of any other person Grace would have inquired, 'What troubles?' Her silence and want of sympathy spoke volumes, but awoke no surprise in her sister. Her wonder was that no one but herself seemed to have any suspicion of Edward Roscoe in connection with the disappearance of her sister. To her mind his very face—for she had spoken less than the truth when she said, 'You will see some change in him'—was a self-accusation of crime. His hollow eyes illumined by strange fires (like natural caverns shown to visitors), his sunken cheeks, his listening and distracted air, were to her fancy so many witnesses against him; yet, ghost of his former self as he was, she did not pity him, and felt as if she never should. In this last conviction she was, however, mistaken. She had gone to him at his desire that morning to acquaint him with the result of his application to see Grace.

'She will see you at half-past two,' she said. 'You must not talk to her on any exciting subject. The interview must not last beyond five minutes. The nurse will be in the next room, and will come in at the expiration of that time.'

All this was said mechanically, as if learned by rote and spoken to a stranger; but she was satisfied with the performance of her task. She had at least shown no sign of the horror and loathing with which she regarded him. And he, too, had seemed satisfied, for indeed he now expected little from her. It was something that she could command herself, which, when they were alone together, was by no means always the case. She would give way to remorse, despair, and hysterical sobbings, to stop which neither menace nor arguments—blandishments he dared not use, she shrank from them as though he were a leper—were of any avail.

'I will come to you,' he said, 'at the appointed time, if you will be my usher.'

But she saw him before that.

She had been despatched by the Doctor to administer Grace's tonic to her that forenoon, and was on her way to Agnes's room to fetch it, when she met her husband face to face at the very door. He was coming out as she was going into the room, and they both started back in amazement and alarm. It was not a place in which either of them was likely to find the other, for it was hateful to both of them; but Philippa, as has been said, had business there.

'I came for a book,' he said, in dry, hoarse tones, in answer to her wondering glance, 'but could not find it.' It was strange that he could not also find a less transparent excuse for what he had not been accused of, but Edward Roscoe was not himself. Nor, even of late days, had he ever looked so unlike himself. His face was livid, his eyes were wild and bloodshot.

'What is the matter?' inquired Philippa, terrified for the moment by his appearance out of the utter indifference to his well-being or otherwise that had taken possession of her.

'Nothing. You had better ask no questions. All you have henceforth to do is to hold your tongue. Forget everything else and remember *that*.'

The words were spoken like the flick of a whip, and there had been a time when they would have silenced her; but her fear of him, strangely enough, was half overcome by her fear *for* him. She was convinced that he was about to do something desperate, and, as she thought, to himself. This man was after all her husband

'Edward, what are you thinking of? Do not look at me like that. It is possible to make matters even worse than they are.'

'They must be worse before they are better,' he answered coldly. 'Leave *me* alone, and I will leave *you* alone.' She was moving after him as fast as her trembling limbs would permit her; he turned round and faced her with a mocking smile. 'You had better not; I am going somewhere where you would not like to follow me.' He passed through the door that shut off the corridor from the narrow staircase and locked it behind him.

A few minutes afterwards Philippa, with head uncovered, was running through the thick falling snow to the 'Cottage,' crying, 'Richard! Richard!'

Richard Roscoe met her in the lobby.

'Your brother has left the house,' she cried in pitiful tones. 'For heaven's sake follow him; I fear he will do himself a mischief.'

'I think not,' he answered dryly. 'Let me know exactly what has happened.'

She told him what had actually taken place, for, indeed, she had no wits left to conceal, far less to invent, anything. 'I met him coming out of Agnes's sitting-room, looking like a madman. He said he was going somewhere where I dared not follow him—and he is gone.'

'Was that all?' inquired the other cynically, when Philippa stopped for want of breath.

'Alas! no, it was not all. When I opened the medicine chest in Agnes's room to get her tonic as the Doctor had told me to do—it is strychnine, you know—the bottle was gone.'

'The strychnine!' cried Richard with sudden excitement; 'what did he want that for?'

'Ah, what indeed? It could only be for one purpose.'

'Which way did he go?' inquired Richard hurriedly. 'Is he upstairs or down?'

'He is gone out, I tell you. I saw him, through the window, going towards the lake.'

Richard reached down his wideawake from the peg in the lobby.

'You must not go out like that in this snow,' cried Philippa with nervous carefulness;

'you will catch your death of cold. Let me help you with your great-coat.'

'Are you *sure* he went out of doors?' asked Richard as he drew it on.

'I am quite sure.'

'Well, well, I'll follow,' said the other. But he was no longer in such hot haste. His apprehensions, which had seemed so keen, had unaccountably subsided. 'Perhaps he is in the summer-house on the terrace.'

'Oh, no, I should think not,' she answered faintly.

'Why not? It is the only place under cover. Well, I'll find him. In return, however, promise me *this*—that until I come back again the nurse shall never leave your sister's room.'

'She never does leave it.'

'She left it yesterday,' he answered bluntly, 'when Sinclair was with her.'

'Walter is different, you know,' said Philippa, with a feeble smile. 'Nobody else would be admitted unless the nurse were present. Those were the Doctor's orders.'

'Never mind his orders; I want your promise that it shall be so.' His tone was fierce; his manner for the first time reminded her of his brother crossed.

'Indeed I will see to that, Mr. Richard,' she answered humbly and amazed, 'upon my honour.'

He nodded, and, pressing his cap over his brows, went out into the whirling snow.

Philippa returned at once to Grace's room. She had resolved to stay there herself till she should have news from Richard. His words had added a vague alarm to her fears on Edward's account, notwithstanding that the two were somehow incompatible. Though in perfect health, and with wealth, as her husband had assured her for her comfort (though it had given her none), beyond the dreams of avarice, there was no more miserable woman in all the world. How infinitely to be envied was her sister, though enervated by sickness, and with no brilliant prospect before her! She was about to marry the man of her choice; ignorant of evil schemes and plans, far less of crime; full of hope and trust; grateful even for ministrations from a hand that had helped to harm her.

'What is the matter, Philippa?' for with returning health her eye had resumed its keenness for the signs of unhappiness in others.

'Nothing, dear; that is, I am a little anxious because Mr. Roscoe and his brother are out in this dreadful snow.'

'That is surely very imprudent of Mr. Richard,' observed Grace. Her sympathies, it seemed, did not extend to his brother. Then presently, 'I hope Agnes is really better; I have not seen her for so many days. Sometimes I fear that she does not want to see me.'

'She would come if she could, dear Grace—

of that you may be certain,' said Philippa earnestly.

'Have you seen her this morning?'

'I had only just left her room when I came into yours.' To have to give such replies to such questions had been long the duty of those who attended Grace's sick-room. They had got used to the practice of duplicity; though it was always dreadful to Philippa to have to speak of Agnes, there was just now another weight upon her mind even more oppressive. Her words were mechanical, and gave her little pain.

'There is the luncheon gong, dear Philippa; I must insist on your going downstairs to the others; you are moping yourself to death up here. Nurse will take good care of me—though indeed I now hardly want anyone.'

Philippa was very willing to go, for anxiety to know whether the brothers had returned consumed her; but before doing so she laid strict injunctions on the nurse not to leave the invalid till she returned.

'I am not in the habit of leaving my patients, madam,' was the tart reply. Sick nurses are angels nowadays, but their wings are of delicate texture, and they must not be 'sat upon.'

'My sister had a reason, nurse,' interposed Grace sweetly, 'and I am grateful to her, though you are quite right too. You would not leave me alone with any visitor, I know.'

Then the other two understood that the idea of the interview with Mr. Roscoe was weighing on her mind.

CHAPTER LI

PHILIPPA SPEAKS OUT

THE luncheon-table at Halswater Hall had of late been but sparely patronised, but the guests were now few indeed; Mr. Allerton and Walter were the only ones that Philippa found there. Places, indeed, were laid for the two brothers, but they had not yet come in, though none but herself entertained any serious apprehensions on their account.

'Why people in the country go out in weather that they would not dream of exposing themselves to in town,' remarked the lawyer, helping himself to pigeon pie, 'is always a riddle to me without an answer. It can't be for appetite, for though I have been writing all the morning I am quite as hungry as if I had been wet through or frozen. Why *do* they do it?'

'There is no harm in it if one is strong and well,' observed Walter; 'but for Mr. Richard to have gone out on such a day as this is certainly very imprudent. Don't you think so, Miss Philippa?'

'No doubt it is; and I am sorry to say it is I who was the cause of it,' was the unexpected reply.

Remorse, or perhaps the 'late beginnings' of a resolve to be frank and open in the future in all things permissible, had moved her to the confession, yet no sooner was it made than she repented of it. She perceived too late that her words required an explanation; her companions, indeed, were obviously waiting for it.

'I had seen Mr. Roscoe in the garden, and I begged his brother to fetch him in,' she added, after a pause.

'In the garden, in a snowstorm!' ejaculated the lawyer. 'You should have sent him out a strait-waistcoat with " Miss Philippa's compliments, and the padded room was being prepared for him." What on earth can they be doing, do you suppose? Gardening?'

There was a look on Philippa's face that checked Walter's answering smile.

'If they do not return in five minutes,' he said gravely, 'I will go out and seek for them.'

'Madman No. 3,' observed the lawyer.

There really seemed no possibility of their having come to harm, though it must be admitted that, if there had been, the speaker would have borne it with equanimity. He detested Edward, and knew nothing of Richard except that he was Edward's brother.

'There is the front door bell!' cried Philippa, starting to her feet. 'They have come back.' And with that she hurried from the room.

'Everybody is mad to-day!' exclaimed the lawyer. 'If Roscoe has come back, why should Miss Philippa suppose he would ring the bell? It is not his way in his own house.'

'I am really afraid there is something wrong,' said Walter; 'I know what a snow-storm is in this region.'

'And yet you are going out in it?'

'I have promised,' was the other's quiet reply, as he rose from the table.

'Very good,' answered the lawyer grudgingly; 'only remember there is some one interested in your welfare, which, as far as I know, is not the case with the other two gentlemen.'

The visitor turned out to be the Doctor, who had come long before his time because of the snowstorm.

'It was a case of now or never,' he said to Philippa, who received, though it could hardly be said welcomed, him. Her anxiety about the brothers was getting overwhelming. What *could* have happened?

'Every hour makes travelling more difficult. It is weather in which one would not turn out a curlew; nobody could stand it but a country doctor. Well,' as Philippa led the way upstairs, ' how is your sister ? '

' Progressing, I think, though she seemed a little depressed this morning.'

' Depressed! That should not have been. She had her tonic, I suppose, as I directed ? '

' No, she did not.'

In spite of her new-born resolutions Philippa would have evaded the question had it been possible; but to have been caught out in a falsehood about the matter—which was almost certain to happen—would have been dangerous indeed.

' She did not? And why not ? '

The Doctor had stopped short in his march along the corridor, and put the question with some energy. He was a great stickler for medical authority, and especially his own authority.

'I could not find the bottle,' she murmured.

'Not find the bottle? This must be inquired into at once, Miss Philippa. It contained, as I told you, strychnine, a deadly poison, and should be always kept under lock and key.'

They were standing opposite the door of Agnes's room, and the Doctor entered it at once. The medicine-chest, a highly ornamented affair, stood on a bracket, with the key in it.

'You surely never left it like that?'

'I am not sure,' she murmured faintly. 'The key ought to have been in my own drawer; but not finding it there when the hour came for giving Grace her tonic, I thought it might be where you now see it. It was there, but the bottle was gone.'

'Yes, madam,' said the Doctor, looking at her with great severity; ' and I perceive that you know who has taken it. It is I who will be held responsible in this matter, and I must insist upon knowing it too.'

'Mr. Roscoe took it.'

'Mr. Roscoe!' The Doctor's face turned suddenly pale; perhaps he had had already his suspicions of Mr. Roscoe, or they had been aroused by Mr. Allerton's views of that gentleman.

'This is a very serious affair, Miss Philippa. I do not leave the house until that bottle is placed in my possession. Where *is* Mr. Roscoe?'

'Would to heaven I knew!' she answered earnestly. 'He has gone out, taking the bottle with him. He has been away for hours in this pitiless snow.'

'Better out than in,' was the Doctor's reflection. The knowledge that the man was absent soothed certain immediate apprehensions that had seized his mind; the sight of Philippa's terror-stricken face filled him with pity for her.

'You think he meant mischief—I mean, of course, to himself—do you? But why should he have gone out of doors?'

'I do not think he knew what he was doing, Doctor. If anything has happened to him, which Heaven forbid, he was not responsible for his actions. He has had much to trouble him of late.'

'Did he go out before lunch?'

'Oh, yes! Long before.'

The question was not asked for the reason that Philippa supposed. The fact has been well ascertained that people do not commit suicide upon empty stomachs.

'Well, well, we must wait and see; your sister, of course, must know nothing of this. Her tonic, if she asks about it, has been intermitted.'

Grace did not ask about it. She was not one of those invalids who are solicitous about their medicine.

'Am I very bad to-day?' she inquired, smiling, noticing the Doctor's serious looks.

'No, miss, you are better, but you must have change of air. The sooner you can get away from this place the better.'

'And poor Agnes, too. She must need it as much as I, by all accounts.'

The Doctor nodded assent. 'When she hears the truth,' he was saying to himself, 'it is probable she will have a relapse.'

True to his promise, he remained at the Hall, and not unwillingly, perhaps, considering the state of the weather, accepted the offer of a bed for the night.

After some hours Walter returned, looking like a snow-man. He had seen nothing of the brothers; they were not in the grounds, nor had anyone the least idea where they could be. Some one had seen them walking together, he said, towards the head of the lake, and thither Walter had gone, but there was no trace of them in that direction. If they had been seen at all, they must have been going the opposite way, towards the post-town. The dinner-party that day included the Doctor, the lawyer, and Walter only, Philippa having declined to appear. The meal was a very silent one till the servants had withdrawn, when the conversation, though gloomy, did not flag. The three men, being of one mind in the main, talked openly with one another.

'The absence of these gentlemen is getting very serious,' said the Doctor. 'Is there any possible explanation of it?' The story of the strychnine, which after all could only affect one of them, he kept to himself.

'I have none,' said Walter. 'I can only say that if they have not been housed somewhere long ere this, I fear it will go hard with them.'

'I will say more than that: in that case they are dead men,' said the Doctor. 'You do not take so serious a view of it, Mr. Allerton?' For, indeed, there was a half-smile on the lawyer's face. 'You do not know what Cumberland is in a snowstorm!'

'I don't know the scene of this drama so well as you do, Doctor,' answered the other dryly; 'but, perhaps, I know one of the characters better. He may have his own reasons for disappearing; but he will have taken care (of that I am certain) of his precious skin.'

'But why should he want to disappear in such an unaccountable fashion?'

'It is one way of settling with one's creditors, and, unless rumour does him wrong, he has a good many. Between ourselves, he has been very hard hit indeed; and as to the fashion, nothing could be better chosen. It makes a clean sweep of the slate. It would never have done if he meant going to go away in a carriage and pair. His position here is not what it was; perhaps he felt that the game was up. And if he has gone, I shall be very much surprised if he has gone empty-handed. What you are saying to yourself I know, Doctor, is, this is a lawyer's view of his fellow-creatures; but I know the man I am talking about.'

'But, my dear Mr. Allerton,' said Walter, 'we have to account for the absence of two men, and not of one.'

'They are two men who are brothers, however; to leave Richard behind him would have been to leave a witness against him who could never stand cross-examination. It is my opinion that they have laid their plans beforehand, and that it is a family affair.'

'There, I would stake my life upon it, Mr. Allerton, you are wrong!' exclaimed Walter earnestly. 'Edward Roscoe may be all you think him to be, but Richard is an honest fellow. He would never be mixed up in anything disgraceful. Moreover, he has not the least sympathy with his brother, and hates his wicked ways.'

'Well, well, we shall see,' said the lawyer, cracking his walnuts. 'There is no one like your scoundrel for putting a fancy value upon his existence, and I have the greatest confidence in Mr. Roscoe's taking care of himself.'

'I agree with you so far,' said the Doctor; and indeed he was quite of opinion that Mr. Roscoe had not taken Miss Grace's tonic for his own use; 'but I have grave fears for the safety of both these gentlemen, nevertheless.'

As time went on and nothing was heard of the missing men, that apprehension became general. The household was plunged in the same state of grim uncertainty that it had been on the occasion of the disappearance of Miss Agnes, but it lasted much longer. There was no key to it, as there had been in the former case.

It was noticed with surprise that Miss Philippa was even more affected by it than she had been at the loss of her sister, but this was in reality because she was seen to be affected. On the other occasion she had withdrawn herself from the rest, whereas she was now always about the house, looking through every window on the snow that still covered the cold earth, and always on the watch for she knew not what. She suffered from insomnia, and began to give the Doctor more anxiety than his other patient, who, indeed, was making rapid progress towards recovery. She had a better tonic than Mr. Roscoe was supposed to have deprived her of in the visits of her lover, and she took them twice a day. Mr. Allerton never wavered in his opinion that the brothers had gone away for reasons of their own; and when their return seemed out of the question he ventured to express his views to Philippa herself.

'It grieves me,' he said, 'to see you so distressed about your missing friends. Dr. Gardner tells me you are fretting about them day and night. I am convinced in my own mind that an explanation is to be found for it.'

'What explanation?' she inquired eagerly.

'Well, it is not a pleasant thing to say of an absent man, but I happen to know that Mr. Roscoe has for a long time been in difficulties; he is unable to meet his engagements, which are very heavy, and has therefore probably run away from them. That is the plain truth.'

He looked for an outburst of indignation, but she shook her head, and answered gently: 'No, it is not that; I know all about his difficulties.'

Mr. Allerton stared. 'The deuce you do!' was what he was saying to himself.

'You are a wise man. Think, think, of some other solution,' she went on in despairing tones. 'Have you no hint, no clue? This suspense is more than I can bear.'

The lawyer looked sharply up at her; he had never had so high an opinion of Mr.

Roscoe's talents as at that moment, nor thought so badly of him.

'We have no clue because we have no data,' he answered. 'If his brother had been left behind we could have examined Mr. Roscoe's papers, but as it is we have no authority to meddle with them.'

'Then I give you that authority, for I am his wife!'

'Good heavens, madam! and how long has that been?'

'We were married before my father's death.'

CHAPTER LII

THE BURNT MILLION

IF the revelation made by Philippa gave the lawyer no immediate clue to the mystery in hand, it made clear another matter which had always puzzled him. Hitherto he could never understand why Mr. Roscoe had not incited the sisters to dispute their father's will. The reason was now plain. Whatever view a judge might have taken against restraint of marriage and in favour of religious liberty, he would certainly have stretched no point for a man who, living under the same roof with her, had clandestinely married his employer's daughter. That Mr. Roscoe had enjoyed—or, at all events, spent—an income to which neither he nor his wife had had any right would, under other circumstances, have been a serious consideration, but just now there were things more pressing. Poor Josh's million would, after Grace's marriage, now belong to the representatives of his faraway cousins, or, failing them, to the national exchequer. It is not possible to describe how the honest old lawyer resented this fact. He almost regretted that he had given his consent to the union of those two young people, for whom he nevertheless felt more affection than for any other of his fellow-creatures. It was really throwing money away—and such a heap of money!

Nevertheless, he not only set to work upon this distasteful matter, but took Walter into his confidence. He was a little disappointed at the lack of interest which the young fellow showed in Philippa's revelation. 'You seem hardly to understand, my young friend, that but for this mad marriage of hers —about which I fear there is little doubt; it was done at the register-office in Kensington, within half a mile of Cedar Lodge—she would have been the richest woman in England; nay, sir—for I must needs be frank with you— I have pointed out to Grace that if she chooses to give you up she may be herself that richest woman.'

'So she told me,' observed Walter dryly.

'Oh, she did, did she? Then I call it a distinct breach of confidence as between ward and guardian.'

'But she also said that you were afraid matters had gone too far between us to admit of her giving me up,' continued Walter, smiling.

'I said I thought you would have ground for an action for breach of promise,' growled the lawyer, 'and that perhaps she would not like to appear in the witness-box; but I wish you to know what she is giving up for you.'

'Indeed, Mr. Allerton,' said Walter gravely, 'I put that matter before her as forcibly as my heart would let me ; though, in giving me herself, she had already given what is worth more than all the wealth in the world. The fact is that she detests the very name of money. Through it, as I gather, she believes her father became the man he was, and indeed, from all I hear, he worshipped it ; through it this unhappy man Roscoe has been tempted to do all sorts of dirty tricks ; through it, and the jealousies and disappointments arising from it, her home, which might otherwise have been such a happy one, has been made a hell ; through it, and the plots and plans to secure it, she was almost separated from the man she loves for ever. It is no wonder that Grace hates money.'

The lawyer listened in silence ; it was not his way to hear money run down (as it often is by those who are very willing to experience its temptations) without pointing out that it may be a blessing instead of a curse, but he had nothing to say for poor Josh's million. In his heart of hearts he suspected that much worse had come of it than even Grace gave it credit for; and besides, it was now passing out of the hands of his clients into those of a stranger.

'I give you my word, Mr. Allerton,' continued Walter, 'that I had a hard matter to persuade her that even the 10,000*l.* her father left her ought not to be given up, because it might originally have been wrung from the widow and the orphan.'

'What infernal nonsense!' ejaculated the lawyer; 'if Josh had not got it, it would have been lost at cards or on the racecourse. Upon my life, even the best of women—but pray go on.'

'I was only going to say that what seems to me the worst thing about Roscoe was his setting poor Grace against her father's memory; to tell her the truth was bad enough, but it seems he invented some hateful lie about his having defrauded my father, which, if, as I understand, you had not set right, would have kept us apart for ever.'

'Yes; that falsehood of Roscoe's puzzles me still; he had generally *something* to go upon, but that must have been pure invention. Well, I want you to be with me while I examine his papers, which may be very queer reading. He was a methodical fellow — a good man of business in his way—and if he has not burnt them, we may find some clue to his disappearance. It's a nasty thing to do, but we shall have to break open his desk.'

'That is rather a strong measure, is it not?'

'No doubt it is; but desperate diseases require desperate remedies. I have his wife's authority to do it.'

Mr. Roscoe's sitting-room was the very abode of neatness. Everything that a man of business could want was there, and in its place. Here the weekly bills of the household were audited and settled, and the tenants came to pay their rents. Huge MS. books with clasps and keys, with letters painted on them, were on the shelves; their proprietor was a man who could have given an account of his stewardship—though it was never demanded of him—down to the last penny. The desk, which Mr. Allerton recognised as having originally belonged to the late Mr. Tremenhere, was an immense structure, as big as a wardrobe. It had held secrets in Josh's time, which the lawyer would have given much to have got hold of; and it doubtless held secrets now. The middle part of it—the desk proper—was that to which he first gave his attention. It was locked, of course, and with no ordinary key; and it took some minutes with hammer and chisel to force it open. It was full of papers, all docketed and arranged with admirable neatness.

'I was wrong,' exclaimed Mr. Allerton, as he cast his eyes over them. 'The man is dead. He would never knowingly have left these proofs behind him.' There were statements of accounts with the two Miss Tremenheres—some of them were memoranda, but all expressed in the most concise and careful manner—which almost made his hair stand on end: huge sums of money, varying from 500*l.* to 5,000*l.*, which had been received from them at different times, and all, no doubt, lost in speculation. On one of them borrowed from Agnes not many weeks before was written in pencil the words, 'Very difficult'; there was no such note to Philippa's loans, which were much more numerous and larger. 'What an insatiable scoundrel!' muttered the lawyer; 'and I have no doubt that he spent every shilling on himself.'

'There is a letter to Richard with an American post-mark,' observed Walter, who was looking over the other's shoulder; 'I wonder how *that* came into Mr. Roscoe's desk.'

'I am afraid we have no business with it,' said the lawyer doubtfully.

'I am quite sure Mr. Roscoe had none,' replied Walter. 'Richard has had no letter, as he told me himself, poor fellow, bitterly enough, since he came to England; and his brother keeps the bag.'

'Judas!' muttered Mr. Allerton, and tore open the document. 'Great heavens! this is news indeed!'

'What have you found?'

For a moment the lawyer was unable to answer him. His ordinarily impassive face was full of excitement; his hands trembled as he read.

'This concerns you, my lad; do you know the handwriting?'

'Indeed I do,' cried Walter, greatly moved; 'it is my poor father's.'

It was the document addressed to Walter which Richard had left for safety in America, and had been forwarded to him by his correspondent; it was duly witnessed, and set forth in a simple style that for certain reasons the writer had changed his name of Vernon for Sinclair, and how he had been cheated of his property by his cousin, Joseph Tremenhere. 'I have no wish that you should resume your name, dear boy,' it went on to say, 'and far less nourish animosity against him who wronged me, but I have thought it right that you should know who you really are in case I may not live to tell you, and to acquaint you with my unfortunate history. The man to whom I have entrusted this paper is my dearest friend, and may be thoroughly relied on.'

The frown that had at first settled on Walter's face was now succeeded by a look of the profoundest dejection.

'Then Roscoe spoke the truth to Grace after all,' he sighed.

'Only just as much of it as suited his purpose. I know something you do not know. Walter, I have great news for you. Mr. Tremenhere, no doubt repentant of the wrong he had done your father, made him, under certain conditions, the heir of his whole fortune. These conditions, by the death of one daughter and the marriage of another, have been fulfilled, except as far as Grace is concerned, and now in marrying you she will lose nothing, for the money which she thereby forfeits will revert to yourself. It was the knowledge of this fact thus conveyed that no doubt caused Roscoe, who was previously in favour of your marriage, to oppose himself to it; why he kept such a dangerous secret in his possession it is impossible to tell, but we may be sure he never intended to disclose it, save for reason good. However, it has now fallen into the proper hands. My dear Walter, I congratulate you sincerely ; you are as rich as Crœsus.'

'You mean to say that, thanks to this document, I can become so?'

'Certainly ; it will only be necessary to prove its correctness.'

'And without it?'

'Well, of course nothing could be proved ——Madman! what have you done?'

Walter had suddenly thrown the paper into the fire and set his heel upon it.

'You have burnt a million of money.'

'I have burnt the only evidence of Mr. Tremenhere's fraud,' answered Walter coolly. 'Do you suppose that the ignorance of that miserable fact will not be a greater comfort to her than the reflection that she had all the money in the world? Has her experience of what money can do been likely to induce her to value it?'

The lawyer stared at him with astonishment and horror; he hardly knew what he said; his moral nature—or that second one with which his profession had supplied him—had suffered a serious shock.

'It was too great a sacrifice,' he muttered, as if in protest, 'to be made by any man.'

'At all events,' returned Walter, smiling, 'it was not an unselfish one, since, if Grace knew that her father had robbed mine, I verily believe she would have shrunk from me. She will now never know it. The memory of her father, if it cannot be what it once was to her, will at least be free from disgrace, and she will not, through conscientious (however foolish) scruples, be ashamed to take her husband.'

'There is something in that,' admitted the lawyer ruefully. 'Walter Sinclair—for Sinclair is what you must still be called—you are a fine fellow, and I am proud to call myself your friend. It was a fond and foolish act, but it was a noble one; and, since the mischief is done, perhaps you will be interested to learn that you are a public benefactor : failing your father's heirs, Mr. Tremenhere's money was to go to the Commissioners for the reduction of the National Debt, and now they will have it without even saying " thank you." But at all events we can make them wait. Every week your marriage is postponed Grace will be putting by a thousand pounds or so ; of course your engagement will now be a very long one.

'It will seem so, no doubt,' said Walter, sighing. 'We are to be married in the spring.'

'A very appropriate time, if we are to believe the poets,' said Mr. Allerton cheerfully ; ' but of course you don't mean *next* spring?'

'My good sir, if I had my way, and dear Grace was herself again,' said Walter, 'we should be married to-morrow.'

CHAPTER LIII

PEACE AT LAST

NOTWITHSTANDING Walter's lover-like impatience, or, as Mr. Allerton termed it, his stark, staring madness, his marriage with Grace did not come off till a considerable sum had accumulated for the young people. Events of a very grave nature interposed between the cup and the lip. It had been foreseen, indeed, by Dr. Gardner that the intelligence of the loss of her sister, which had sooner or later to be communicated to her, would have a retarding effect on Grace's recovery, and this turned out to be the case; but there were other circumstances that helped to depress and distress her, and had she not had Walter's love to comfort her and the prospect of a happier future to look forward to, there is little doubt but that their cumulative effect would have proved fatal to a constitution already severely tried.

No news had come to hand of either Mr. Roscoe or his brother; the lake still held the remains of Agnes in its icy grasp; and since it was imperative that Grace should be removed from a spot so full of melancholy associations as Halswater, it was arranged that she should leave home with Philippa (who needed change of scene at least as much as herself) for the Isle of Wight; but this could not be done without awakening suspicions and anxieties that compelled some explanation. Where were those three members of the little household—the sister for whom she still entertained affection, however ill-deserved; the friend of the family whose absence was felt, if not deplored, in all domestic arrangements; and his brother for whom she had entertained so genuine a regard? It was absolutely necessary to tell her why none of them were present to wish her good-bye, and the consequence was that she left home a mourner, and more of an invalid than ever. A house had been secured for the sisters at Ventnor with a large garden overlooking the sea, while Walter took up his quarters in a neighbouring hotel. Notwithstanding what Mr. Allerton persisted in calling his 'gigantic sacrifice' (as if it had been a sale of goods), the course of true love was by no means running smooth. Indeed, at one time Grace's state of health became so serious that it seemed possible that the Burnt Million had been burnt for nothing —an apprehension which, if it did not move him to tears, brought the drops out on the good lawyer's brow.

The land agent at Halswater, whose place it had been Mr. Roscoe's intention that his brother should fill, was instructed to have the lake dragged as soon as the disappearance of the ice permitted, and the first result of that operation at the foot of the terrace walk was startling indeed. The grappling hooks brought to land—not one body, but two, and neither of them that which they sought. They were those of the two brothers, 'clasped,' as the newspaper reports expressed it, 'in one another's arms.' It was supposed to be an affecting incident of fraternal love. Those who knew them well knew better. Mr. Allerton's explanation of the matter, at all events—and I think it was a shrewd one—founded on his own suspicions and on what Philippa and Walter told him, was as follows.

Driven to his wits' end by the failure of his plans and the concealment of a terrible crime, Roscoe had desperately conceived another—the murder of Grace herself; for that purpose, and not for that of self-slaughter, he had obtained the bottle of strychnine which was found in his breast pocket; this conclusion was the very one that Richard arrived at on hearing Philippa's story, and, furious at the danger that threatened Grace, he had sought his brother with the intention of taxing him with this intention and also of obtaining possession of the bottle. He had found him on the terrace walk, on the very spot where a similar catastrophe had occurred to Agnes, and a struggle had ensued in which both brothers had fallen over the cliff. The coroner's jury, however, returned a verdict of 'accidental death' in their case, as in that of Agnes, whose body was found a day or two afterwards, it having drifted for some distance down the lake.

The newspapers were studiously kept from Philippa, but the news had to be told her, and in due time she broke it to Grace. It was no wonder that the poor girl's convalescence was retarded; but in the end youth and love brought her forth from the valley of death.

Walter Sinclair was never suspected of having borne the name of Vernon, nor did that circumstance, since Grace was ignorant

of it, affect the legality of their marriage.
The transference of her father's fortune to the
Commissioners of the National Debt was not
even a nine days' wonder—for who heeds a
drop in the ocean?—except with Mrs. Linden.
That lady never ceased to have an imaginative
interest in Josh's million, and to express her
astonishment that no heirs to Mr. Vernon of
Cockermouth were ever discovered. If she
had been informed on affidavit that any human
being had sacrificed such a sum, on the altar
of Hymen or anywhere else, she would certainly have refused to believe it; but he who
had done the deed never repented of it for an
instant. The young couple have quite as
much money as is good for them, and Grace
can think of him who had been wont to call
her 'his little Fairy,' if not with the old trust
and tenderness, at all events without the flush
of shame. Mr. Allerton, who is a frequent
guest of theirs, and has had many opportuni-
ties of contemplating their happiness, is com-

pelled to own that in surrendering his place among the millionaires of England Walter has found ample compensation.

Philippa—a changed woman, and greatly for the better—resides within a stone's-throw of her married sister in the Isle of Wight, for Halswater Hall, with its sombre memories, has long passed into other hands.

In a fair garden by the sea there is a little toddler who has as yet but a single playmate, one who never quarrels with her or envies her the possession of her many toys. He is almost as great a favourite with her as he is with her father and mother; there is a tender association between them and him of which the child knows nothing. He passes his days on the sunny lawn and his nights in a well-lined basket at the foot of their bed, and, though he knows no more of the Burnt Million than the rest of the world, enjoys his master's fullest confidence and affection. On what slight causes hinge our poor human affairs! 'But for you, Rip,' says Walter gratefully, as he caresses the little creature, 'I should, perhaps, never have won your mistress.'

THE END.

January, 1890.

A LIST OF BOOKS
PUBLISHED BY
CHATTO & WINDUS
214, PICCADILLY, LONDON, W.

Sold by a'l Booksellers, or sent post-free for the published price by the Publishers.

Abbé Constantin (The). By LUDOVIC HALEVY, of the French Academy. Translated into English. With 36 Photogravure Illustrations by GOUPIL & Co., after the Drawings of Madame MADELEINE LEMAIRE. Price may be learned from any Bookseller.

About.—The Fellah: An Egyptian Novel. By EDMOND ABOUT. Translated by Sir RANDAL ROBERTS. Post 8vo, illustrated boards, 2s.; cloth limp, 2s. 6d.

Adams (W. Davenport), Works by:
A Dictionary of the Drama. Being a comprehensive Guide to the Plays, Playwrights, Players, and Playhouses of the United Kingdom and America. Crown 8vo, half-bound, 12s. 6d. [*Preparing.*
Quips and Quiddities. Selected by W. DAVENPORT ADAMS. Post 8vo, cloth limp, 2s. 6d.

Adams (W. H. D.).— Witch, Warlock, and Magician: Historical Sketches of Magic and Witchcraft in England and Scotland. By W. H. DAVENPORT ADAMS. Demy 8vo, cloth extra, 12s.

Agony Column (The) of "The Times," from 1800 to 1870. Edited, with an Introduction, by ALICE CLAY. Post 8vo, cloth limp, 2s. 6d.

Aïdé (Hamilton), Works by:
Post 8vo, illustrated boards, 2s. each.
Carr of Carrlyon. | Confidences.

Alexander (Mrs.), Novels by:
Post 8vo, illustrated boards, 2s. each.
Maid, Wife, or Widow?
Valerie's Fate.

Allen (Grant), Works by:
Crown 8vo, cloth extra, 6s. each.
The Evolutionist at Large.
Vignettes from Nature.
Colin Clout's Calendar.

Crown 8vo, cloth extra, 6s. each; post 8vo, illustrated boards, 2s. each.
Strange Stories. With a Frontispiece by GEORGE DU MAURIER.
The Beckoning Hand. With a Frontispiece by TOWNLEY GREEN.

Crown 8vo, cloth extra, 3s. 6d. each; post 8vo, illustrated boards, 2s. each.
Philistia. | The Devil's Die.
This Mortal Coll.

Post 8vo, illustrated boards, 2s. each.
Babylon: A Romance.
For Malmie's Sake.
In all Shades.

The Tents of Shem. With a Frontispiece by E. F. BREWTNALL. Crown 8vo, cloth extra, 3s. 6d.

Architectural Styles, A Handbook of. Translated from the German of A. ROSENGARTEN, by W. COLLETT-SANDARS. Crown 8vo, cloth extra, with 639 Illustrations, 7s. 6d.

Arnold.—Bird Life in England. By EDWIN LESTER ARNOLD. Crown 8vo, cloth extra, 6s.

Art (The) of Amusing: A Collection of Graceful Arts, Games, Tricks, Puzzles, and Charades. By FRANK BELLEW. With 300 Illustrations. Cr. 8vo, cloth extra, 4s. 6d.

Artemus Ward:

Artemus Ward's Works: The Works of CHARLES FARRER BROWNE, better known as ARTEMUS WARD. With Portrait and Facsimile. Crown 8vo, cloth extra, 7s. 6d.

The Genial Showman: Life and Adventures of Artemus Ward. By EDWARD P. HINGSTON. With a Frontispiece. Cr. 8vo, cl. extra, 3s. 6d.

Ashton (John), Works by:

Crown 8vo, cloth extra, 7s. 6d. each.

A History of the Chap-Books of the Eighteenth Century. With nearly 400 Illustrations, engraved in facsimile of the originals.

Social Life in the Reign of Queen Anne. From Original Sources. With nearly 100 Illustrations.

Humour, Wit, and Satire of the Seventeenth Century. With nearly 100 Illustrations.

English Caricature and Satire on Napoleon the First. With 115 Illustrations.

Modern Street Ballads. With 57 Illustrations

Bacteria.—A Synopsis of the

Bacteria and Yeast Fungi and Allied Species. By W. B. GROVE, B.A. With 87 Illusts. Crown 8vo, cl. extra, 3s. 6d.

Bankers, A Handbook of London;

together with Lists of Bankers from 1677. By F. G. HILTON PRICE. Crown 8vo, cloth extra, 7s. 6d.

Bardsley (Rev. C.W.), Works by:

English Surnames: Their Sources and Significations. Third Edition, revised. Crown 8vo, cl. ex., 7s. 6d.

Curiosities of Puritan Nomenclature. Second Edition. Crown 8vo, cloth extra, 6s.

Baring Gould (S.), Novels by:

Crown 8vo, cloth extra, 3s. 6d. each; post 8vo, illustrated boards, 2s. each.

Red Spider. | Eve.

Barrett.—Fettered for Life.

By FRANK BARRETT, Author of "Lady Biddy Fane," &c. Three Vols., crown 8vo.

Beaconsfield, Lord: A Biography.

By T. P. O'CONNOR, M.P. Sixth Edition, with a New Preface. Crown 8vo, cloth extra, 5s.

Beauchamp. — Grantley

Grange: A Novel. By SHELSLEY BEAUCHAMP. Post 8vo, illust. bds., 2s.

Beautiful Pictures by British

Artists: A Gathering of Favourites from our Picture Galleries. All engraved on Steel in the highest style of Art. Edited, with Notices of the Artists, by SYDNEY ARMYTAGE, M.A. Imperial 4to, cloth extra, gilt and gilt edges, 21s.

Bechstein. — As Pretty as

Seven, and other German Stories. Collected by LUDWIG BECHSTEIN. With Additional Tales by the Brothers GRIMM, and 100 Illusts. by RICHTER. Small 4to, green and gold, 6s. 6d.; gilt edges, 7s. 6d.

Beerbohm. — Wanderings in

Patagonia; or, Life among the Ostrich Hunters. By JULIUS BEERBOHM. With Illusts. Crown 8vo, cloth extra, 3s. 6d.

Bennett (W.C.,LL.D.), Works by:

Post 8vo, cloth limp, 2s. each.

A Ballad History of England.

Songs for Sailors.

Besant (Walter) and James

Rice, Novels by. Crown 8vo, cloth extra, 3s. 6d. each; post 8vo, illust. bds., 2s. each; cl. limp, 2s. 6d. each.

Ready-Money Mortiboy.
My Little Girl.
With Harp and Crown.
This Son of Vulcan.
The Golden Butterfly.
The Monks of Thelema.
By Celia's Arbour.
The Chaplain of the Fleet.
The Seamy Side.
The Case of Mr. Lucraft, &c.
'Twas in Trafalgar's Bay, &c.
The Ten Years' Tenant, &c.

Besant (Walter), Novels by:

Crown 8vo, cloth extra, 3s. 6d. each; post 8vo, illust. boards, 2s. each; cloth limp, 2s. 6d. each.

All Sorts and Conditions of Men: An Impossible Story. With Illustrations by FRED. BARNARD.

The Captains' Room, &c. With Frontispiece by E. J. WHEELER.

All in a Garden Fair. With 6 Illustrations by HARRY FURNISS.

Dorothy Forster. With Frontispiece by CHARLES GREEN.

Uncle Jack, and other Stories.

Children of Gibeon.

The World Went Very Well Then. With Illustrations by A. FORESTIER.

Herr Paulus: His Rise, his Greatness, and his Fall.

CHATTO & WINDUS, PICCADILLY. 3

BESANT (WALTER), continued—
For Faith and Freedom. With Illustrations by A. FORESTIER and F. WADDY. Crown 8vo, cloth extra, 3s. 6d.
To Call her Mine, &c. With Nine Illustrations by A. FORESTIER. Cr. 8vo, cloth extra, 6s.
The Holy Rose, &c. With a Frontispiece by F. BARNARD. Crown 8vo, cloth extra, 6s. [Shortly.
The Bell of St. Paul's. Three Vols., crown 8vo.
Fifty Years Ago. With 137 full-page Plates and Woodcuts. Demy 8vo, cloth extra, 16s.
The Eulogy of Richard Jefferies. With Photograph Portrait. Second Edition. Cr. 8vo, cloth extra, 6s.
The Art of Fiction. Demy 8vo, 1s.

New Library Edition of
Besant and Rice's Novels.
The whole 12 Volumes, printed from new type on a large crown 8vo page, and handsomely bound in cloth, are now ready, price Six Shillings each.
1. Ready-Money Mortiboy. With Etched Portrait of JAMES RICE.
2. My Little Girl.
3. With Harp and Crown.
4. This Son of Vulcan.
5. The Golden Butterfly. With Etched Portrait of WALTER BESANT.
6. The Monks of Thelema.
7. By Celia's Arbour.
8. The Chaplain of the Fleet.
9. The Seamy Side.
10. The Case of Mr. Lucraft, &c.
11. 'Twas in Trafalgar's Bay, &c.
12. The Ten Years' Tenant, &c.

Betham-Edwards (M)—Felicia.
By M. BETHAM-EDWARDS. Cr. 8vo, cloth extra, 3s. 6d.; post 8vo, illust. bds., 2s.

Bewick (Thomas) and his Pupils. By AUSTIN DOBSON. With 95 Illusts. Square 8vo, cloth extra, 6s.

Blackburn's (Henry) Art Handbooks:
Academy Notes, separate years, from 1875 to 1887, and 1889, each 1s.
Academy Notes, 1890. With numerous Illustrations. 1s. [Preparing.
Academy Notes, 1875-79. Complete in One Volume, with about 600 Illustrations. Cloth limp, 6s.
Academy Notes, 1880-84. Complete in One Volume, with about 700 Illustrations. Cloth limp, 6s.
Grosvenor Notes, 1877. 6d.
Grosvenor Notes, separate years, from 1878 to 1889, each 1s.
Grosvenor Notes, 1890. With numerous Illusts. 1s. [Preparing.

BLACKBURN (HENRY), continued—
Grosvenor Notes, Vol. I., 1877-82. With upwards of 300 Illustrations. Demy 8vo, cloth limp, 6s.
Grosvenor Notes, Vol. II., 1883-87. With upwards of 300 Illustrations. Demy 8vo, cloth limp, 6s.
The New Gallery, 1888 and 1889. With numerous Illusts., each 1s.
The New Gallery, 1890. With numerous Illustrations. 1s. [Preparing.
English Pictures at the National Gallery. 114 Illustrations. 1s.
Old Masters at the National Gallery. 128 Illustrations. 1s. 6d.
An Illustrated Catalogue to the National Gallery. With Notes by H. BLACKBURN, and 242 Illustrations. Demy 8vo, cloth limp, 3s.

The Paris Salon, 1890. With 300 Facsimile Sketches. 3s. [Preparing.

Blake (William): Etchings from his Works. By W. B. SCOTT. With descriptive Text. Folio, half-bound boards, India Proofs, 21s.

Blind.—The Ascent of Man:
A Poem. By MATHILDE BLIND. Crown 8vo, printed on hand-made paper, cloth extra, 5s.

Bourne (H. R. Fox), Works by:
English Merchants: Memoirs in Illustration of the Progress of British Commerce. With numerous Illustrations. Cr. 8vo, cloth extra, 7s. 6d.
English Newspapers: Chapters in the History of Journalism. Two Vols., demy 8vo, cloth extra, 25s.

Bowers'(G.) Hunting Sketches:
Oblong 4to, half-bound boards, 21s. each.
Canters in Crampshire.
Leaves from a Hunting Journal. Coloured in facsimile of the originals.

Boyle (Frederick), Works by:
Crown 8vo, cloth extra, 3s. 6d. each; post 8vo, illustrated boards, 2s. each.
Camp Notes: Stories of Sport and Adventure in Asia, Africa, America.
Savage Life: Adventures of a Globe-Trotter.

Chronicles of No-Man's Land. Post 8vo, illust. boards, 2s.

Brand's Observations on Popular Antiquities, chiefly Illustrating the Origin of our Vulgar Customs, Ceremonies, and Superstitions. With the Additions of S.r HENRY ELLIS, and numerous Illustrations. Crown 8vo, cloth extra, 7s. 6d

BOOKS PUBLISHED BY

Bret Harte, Works by:
LIBRARY EDITION, Complete in Five Vols., cr. 8vo, cl. extra, 6s. each.
Bret Harte's Collected Works: LIBRARY EDITION. Arranged and Revised by the Author.
Vol. I. COMPLETE POETICAL AND DRAMATIC WORKS. With Steel Portrait, and Introduction by Author.
Vol. II. EARLIER PAPERS—LUCK OF ROARING CAMP, and other Sketches—BOHEMIAN PAPERS — SPANISH AND AMERICAN LEGENDS.
Vol. III. TALES OF THE ARGONAUTS—EASTERN SKETCHES.
Vol. IV. GABRIEL CONROY.
Vol. V. STORIES — CONDENSED NOVELS, &C.

The Select Works of Bret Harte, in Prose and Poetry. With Introductory Essay by J. M. BELLEW, Portrait of the Author, and 50 Illustrations. Crown 8vo, cloth extra, 7s. 6d.

Bret Harte's Complete Poetical Works. Author's Copyright Edition. Printed on hand-made paper and bound in buckram. Cr. 8vo, 4s. 6d.

The Queen of the Pirate Isle. With 28 original Drawings by KATE GREENAWAY, reproduced in Colours by EDMUND EVANS. Sm. 4to, bds., 5s.

A Waif of the Plains. With 60 Illustrations by STANLEY L. WOOD. Cr. 8vo, cloth extra, 3s. 6d. [*Shortly.*

Post 8vo, illustrated boards, 2s. each.
Gabriel Conroy.
An Heiress of Red Dog, &c.
The Luck of Roaring Camp, and other Sketches.
Californian Stories (including THE TWINS OF TABLE MOUNTAIN, JEFF BRIGGS'S LOVE STORY, &c.)

Post 8vo, illustrated boards, 2s. each; cloth, 2s. 6d. each.
Flip. | Maruja.
A Phyllis of the Sierras.

Fcap. 8vo, picture cover, 1s. each.
The Twins of Table Mountain.
Jeff Briggs's Love Story.

Brewer (Rev. Dr.), Works by:
The Reader's Handbook of Allusions, References, Plots, and Stories. 15th Thousand. With Appendix, containing a COMPLETE ENGLISH BIBLIOGRAPHY. Cr. 8vo, cloth 7s. 6d.
Authors and their Works, with the Dates: Being the Appendices to "The Reader's Handbook," separately printed. Cr. 8vo, cloth limp, 2s.
A Dictionary of Miracles: Imitative, Realistic, and Dogmatic. Crown 8vo, cloth extra, 7s. 6d.

Brewster (Sir David), Works by:
Post 8vo, cloth extra, 4s. 6d. each.
More Worlds than One: The Creed of the Philosopher and the Hope of the Christian. With Plates.
The Martyrs of Science: Lives of GALILEO, TYCHO BRAHE, and KEPLER. With Portraits.
Letters on Natural Magic. A New Edition, with numerous Illustrations, and Chapters on the Being and Faculties of Man, and Additional Phenomena of Natural Magic, by J. A. SMITH.

Brillat-Savarin.—Gastronomy as a Fine Art. By BRILLAT-SAVARIN. Translated by R. E. ANDERSON, M.A. Post 8vo, printed on laid-paper and half-bound, 2s.

Brydges. — Uncle Sam at Home. By HAROLD BRYDGES. Post 8vo, illust. boards, 2s.; cloth, 2s. 6d.

Buchanan's (Robert) Works:
Crown 8vo, cloth extra, 6s. each.
Selected Poems of Robert Buchanan. With a Frontispiece by T. DALZIEL.
The Earthquake; or, Six Days and a Sabbath.
The City of Dream: An Epic Poem. With Two Illustrations by P. MACNAB. Second Edition.

Robert Buchanan's Complete Poetical Works. With Steel-plate Portrait. Crown 8vo, cloth extra, 7s. 6d.

Crown 8vo, cloth extra, 3s. 6d. each; post 8vo, illust. boards, 2s. each.
The Shadow of the Sword.
A Child of Nature. With a Frontispiece.
God and the Man. With Illustrations by FRED. BARNARD.
The Martyrdom of Madeline. With Frontispiece by A. W. COOPER.
Love Me for Ever. With a Frontispiece by P. MACNAB.
Annan Water. | The New Abelard.
Foxglove Manor.
Matt: A Story of a Caravan.
The Master of the Mine.
The Heir of Linne.

Burton (Captain).—The Book of the Sword: Being a History of the Sword and its Use in all Countries, from the Earliest Times. By RICHARD F. BURTON. With over 400 Illustrations. Square 8vo, cloth extra, 32s.

CHATTO & WINDUS, PICCADILLY.   5

Burton (Robert):
The Anatomy of Melancholy. A New Edition, complete, corrected and enriched by Translations of the Classical Extracts. Demy 8vo, cloth extra, 7s. 6d.
Melancholy Anatomised: Being an Abridgment, for popular use, of BURTON'S ANATOMY OF MELANCHOLY. Post 8vo, cloth limp, 2s. 6d.

Caine (T. Hall), Novels by:
Crown 8vo, cloth extra, 3s. 6d. each; post 8vo, illustrated boards, 2s. each.
The Shadow of a Crime.
A Son of Hagar.
The Deemster: A Romance of the Isle of Man.

Cameron (Commander).—
The Cruise of the "Black Prince" Privateer. By V. LOVETT CAMERON, R.N., C.B. With Two Illustrations by P. MACNAB. Crown 8vo, cl. ex., 5s.; post 8vo, illustrated boards, 2s.

Cameron (Mrs. H. Lovett), Novels by:
Crown 8vo, cloth extra, 3s. 6d. each; post 8vo, illustrated boards, 2s. each.
Juliet's Guardian. | Deceivers Ever.

Carlyle (Thomas):
On the Choice of Books. By THOMAS CARLYLE. With a Life of the Author by R. H. SHEPHERD, and Three Illustrations. Post 8vo, cloth extra, 1s. 6d.
The Correspondence of Thomas Carlyle and Ralph Waldo Emerson, 1834 to 1872. Edited by CHARLES ELIOT NORTON. With Portraits. Two Vols., crown 8vo, cloth extra, 24s.

Chapman's (George) Works:
Vol. I. contains the Plays complete, including the doubtful ones. Vol. II., the Poems and Minor Translations, with an Introductory Essay by ALGERNON CHARLES SWINBURNE. Vol. III., the Translations of the Iliad and Odyssey. Three Vols., crown 8vo, cloth extra, 18s.; or separately, 6s. each.

Chatto & Jackson.—A Treatise on Wood Engraving, Historical and Practical. By WM. ANDREW CHATTO and JOHN JACKSON. With an Additional Chapter by HENRY G. BOHN; and 450 fine Illustrations. A Reprint of the last Revised Edition. Large 4to, half-bound, 28s.

Chaucer:
Chaucer for Children: A Golden Key. By Mrs. H.R. HAWEIS. With Eight Coloured Pictures and numerous Woodcuts by the Author. New Ed., small 4to, cloth extra, 6s.
Chaucer for Schools. By Mrs. H. R. HAWEIS. Demy 8vo, cloth limp, 2s. 6d.

Clare.—For the Love of a Lass:
A Tale of Tynedale. By AUSTIN CLARE, Author of "A Child of the Menhir," &c. Two Vols., small 8vo, cloth extra, 12s.

Clodd.— Myths and Dreams.
By EDWARD CLODD, F.R.A.S., Author of "The Story of Creation," &c. Crown 8vo, cloth extra, 5s.

Cobban.—The Cure of Souls:
A Story. By J. MACLAREN COBBAN. Post 8vo, illustrated boards, 2s.

Coleman (John), Works by:
Players and Playwrights I have Known. Two Vols., demy 8vo, cloth extra, 24s.
Curly: An Actor's Romance. With Illustrations by J. C. DOLLMAN. Crown 8vo, cloth, 1s. 6d.

Collins (C. Allston).—The Bar Sinister: A Story. By C. ALLSTON COLLINS. Post 8vo, illustrated bds., 2s.

Collins (Churton).—A Monograph on Dean Swift. By J. CHURTON COLLINS. Crown 8vo, cloth extra, 8s. [*Shortly.*

Collins (Mortimer), Novels by :
Crown 8vo, cloth extra, 3s. 6d. each; post 8vo, illustrated boards, 2s. each.
Sweet Anne Page.
Transmigration.
From Midnight to Midnight.

A Fight with Fortune. Post 8vo, illustrated boards, 2s.

Collins (Mortimer & Frances), Novels by :
Crown 8vo, cloth extra, 3s. 6d. each; post 8vo, illustrated boards, 2s. each.
Blacksmith and Scholar.
The Village Comedy.
You Play Me False.

Post 8vo, illustrated boards, 2s. each.
Sweet and Twenty.
Frances.

Collins (Wilkie), Novels by:
Crown 8vo, cloth extra, 3s. 6d. each;
post 8vo, illustrated boards, 2s. each;
cloth limp, 2s. 6d. each.
Antonina. Illust. by Sir JOHN GILBERT.
Basil. Illustrated by Sir JOHN GILBERT and J MAHONEY.
Hide and Seek. Illustrated by Sir JOHN GILBERT and J. MAHONEY.
The Dead Secret. Illustrated by Sir JOHN GILBERT.
Queen of Hearts. Illustrated by Sir JOHN GILBERT
My Miscellanies. With a Steel-plate Portrait of WILKIE COLLINS.
The Woman In White. With Illustrations by Sir JOHN GILBERT and F. A. FRASER.
The Moonstone. With Illustrations by G. DU MAURIER and F. A. FRASER.
Man and Wife. Illusts. by W. SMALL.
Poor Miss Finch. Illustrated by G. DU MAURIER and EDWARD HUGHES.
Miss or Mrs.? With Illustrations by S. L. FILDES and HENRY WOODS.
The New Magdalen. Illustrated by G. DU MAURIER and C. S. REINHARDT.
The Frozen Deep. Illustrated by G. DU MAURIER and J. MAHONEY.
The Law and the Lady. Illustrated by S. L. FILDES and SYDNEY HALL.
The Two Destinies.
The Haunted Hotel. Illustrated by ARTHUR HOPKINS.
The Fallen Leaves.
Jezebel's Daughter.
The Black Robe.
Heart and Science: A Story of the Present Time.
"I Say No."
The Evil Genius.
Little Novels. | A Rogue's Life.
The Legacy of Cain. Crown 8vo, cloth extra, 3s. 6d.
Blind Love. With a Preface by WALTER BESANT, and 36 Illustrations by A. FORESTIER. Three Vols., crown 8vo.

Colman's Humorous Works:
"Broad Grins," "My Nightgown and Slippers," and other Humorous Works, Prose and Poetical, of GEORGE COLMAN. With Life by G. B BUCKSTONE, and Frontispiece by HOGARTH. Crown 8vo, cloth extra, 7s. 6d.

Colquhoun.—Every Inch a Soldier: A Novel. By M. J. COLQUHOUN. Post 8vo, illustrated boards, 2s.

Convalescent Cookery: A Family Handbook. By CATHERINE RYAN. Crown 8vo, 1s.; cloth, 1s. 6d.

Conway (Moncure D.), Works by:
Demonology and Devil-Lore. Third Edition. With 65 Illustrations. Two Vols., 8vo, cloth extra, 28s.
A Necklace of Stories. Illustrated by W. J. HENNESSY. Square 8vo, cloth extra, 6s.
Pine and Palm: A Novel. Cheaper Ed. Post 8vo, illust. bds., 2s. [Shortly.

Cook (Dutton), Novels by:
Leo. Post 8vo, illustrated boards, 2s.
Paul Foster's Daughter. Crown 8vo, cloth extra, 3s. 6d.; post 8vo, illustrated boards, 2s.

Copyright.—A Handbook of English and Foreign Copyright in Literary and Dramatic Works. By SIDNEY JERROLD. Post 8vo, cl., 2s. 6d.

Cornwall.—Popular Romances of the West of England; or, The Drolls, Traditions, and Superstitions of Old Cornwall. Collected and Edited by ROBERT HUNT, F.R.S. With Two Steel-plate Illustrations by GEORGE CRUIKSHANK. New and Revised Edition, with Additions, crown 8vo, cloth extra, 7s. 6d.

Craddock.—The Prophet of the Great Smoky Mountains. By CHARLES EGBERT CRADDOCK. Post 8vo, illust. bds., 2s.; cloth limp, 2s. 6d.

Cruikshank (George):
The Comic Almanack. Complete in Two SERIES: The FIRST from 1835 to 1843; the SECOND from 1844 to 1853. A Gathering of the BEST HUMOUR of THACKERAY, HOOD, MAYHEW, ALBERT SMITH, A'BECKETT, ROBERT BROUGH, &c. With 2,000 Woodcuts and Steel Engravings by CRUIKSHANK, HINE, LANDELLS, &c. Crown 8vo, cloth gilt, two thick volumes, 7s. 6d. each.
The Life of George Cruikshank. By BLANCHARD JERROLD, Author of "The Life of Napoleon III.," &c. With 84 Illustrations. New and Cheaper Edition, with Additional Plates, and a Bibliography. Crown 8vo, cloth extra, 7s. 6d.

Cumming (C. F. Gordon), Works by:
Demy 8vo, cloth extra, 8s. 6d. each.
In the Hebrides. With Autotype Facsimile and numerous full-page Illusts.
In the Himalayas and on the Indian Plains. With numerous Illusts.

Via Cornwall to Egypt. With a Photogravure Frontispiece. Demy 8vo, cloth extra, 7s. 6d.

Curzon.—The Blue Ribbon of the Turf. By LOUIS HENRY CURZON. Crown 8vo, cloth extra, 6s. [*April.*

Cussans.—Handbook of Heraldry; with Instructions for Tracing Pedigrees and Deciphering Ancient MSS., &c. By JOHN E. CUSSANS. New and Revised Edition, illustrated with over 400 Woodcuts and Coloured Plates. Crown 8vo, cloth extra, 7s. 6d.

Cyples.—Hearts of Gold: A Novel. By WILLIAM CYPLES. Crown 8vo, cloth extra, 3s. 6d.; post 8vo, illustrated boards, 2s.

Daniel.—Merrie England in the Olden Time. By GEORGE DANIEL. With Illustrations by ROBT. CRUIKSHANK. Crown 8vo, cloth extra, 3s. 6d.

Daudet.—The Evangelist; or, Port Salvation. By ALPHONSE DAUDET. Translated by C. HARRY MELTZER. With Portrait of the Author. Crown 8vo, cloth extra, 3s. 6d.; post 8vo, illust. boards, 2s.

Davenant.—Hints for Parents on the Choice of a Profession or Trade for their Sons. By FRANCIS DAVENANT, M.A. Post 8vo, 1s.; cloth limp, 1s. 6d.

Davies (Dr. N. E.), Works by:
Crown 8vo, 1s. each; cloth, 1s. 6d. each.
One Thousand Medical Maxims.
Nursery Hints: A Mother's Guide.
Foods for the Fat: A Treatise on Corpulency, and a Dietary for its Cure.

Aids to Long Life. Crown 8vo, 2s.; cloth limp, 2s. 6d.

Davies' (Sir John) Complete Poetical Works, including Psalms I. to L. in Verse, and other hitherto Unpublished MSS., for the first time Collected and Edited, with Memorial-Introduction and Notes, by the Rev. A. B. GROSART, D.D. Two Vols., crown 8vo, cloth boards, 12s.

De Maistre.—A Journey Round My Room. By XAVIER DE MAISTRE. Translated by HENRY ATTWELL. Post 8vo, cloth limp, 2s. 6d.

De Mille.—A Castle in Spain: A Novel. By JAMES DE MILLE. With a Frontispiece. Crown 8vo, cloth extra, 3s. 6d.; post 8vo, illust. bds., 2s.

Derwent (Leith), Novels by:
Crown 8vo, cloth extra, 3s. 6d. each; post 8vo, illustrated boards, 2s. each.
Our Lady of Tears. | Circe's Lovers.

Dickens (Charles), Novels by:
Post 8vo, illustrated boards, 2s. each.
Sketches by Boz. | Nicholas Nickleby.
Pickwick Papers. | Oliver Twist.

The Speeches of Charles Dickens, 1841-1870. With a New Bibliography, revised and enlarged. Edited and Prefaced by RICHARD HERNE SHEPHERD. Cr. 8vo, cloth extra, 6s.—Also a SMALLER EDITION, in the *Mayfair Library*, post 8vo, cloth limp, 2s. 6d.

About England with Dickens. By ALFRED RIMMER. With 57 Illustrations by C. A. VANDERHOOF, ALFRED RIMMER, and others. Sq. 8vo, cloth extra, 7s. 6d.

Dictionaries:
A Dictionary of Miracles: Imitative, Realistic, and Dogmatic. By the Rev. E. C. BREWER, LL.D. Crown 8vo, cloth extra, 7s. 6d.

The Reader's Handbook of Allusions, References, Plots, and Stories. By the Rev. E. C. BREWER, LL.D. With an Appendix, containing a Complete English Bibliography. Fifteenth Thousand. Crown 8vo, 1,400 pages, cloth extra, 7s. 6d.

Authors and their Works, with the Dates. Being the Appendices to "The Reader's Handbook," separately printed. By the Rev. Dr. BREWER. Crown 8vo, cloth limp, 2s.

A Dictionary of the Drama: Being a comprehensive Guide to the Plays, Playwrights, Players, and Playhouses of the United Kingdom and America, from the Earliest to the Present Times. By W. DAVENPORT ADAMS. A thick volume, crown 8vo, half-bound, 12s. 6d. [*In preparation.*

Familiar Short Sayings of Great Men. With Historical and Explanatory Notes. By SAMUEL A. BENT, M.A. Fifth Edition, revised and enlarged. Cr. 8vo, cloth extra, 7s. 6d.

The Slang Dictionary: Etymological, Historical, and Anecdotal. Crown 8vo, cloth extra, 6s. 6d.

Women of the Day: A Biographical Dictionary. By FRANCES HAYS. Cr. 8vo, cloth extra, 5s.

Words, Facts, and Phrases: A Dictionary of Curious, Quaint, and Out-of-the-Way Matters. By ELIEZER EDWARDS. Crown 8vo, cloth extra, 7s. 6d.

Diderot.—The Paradox of Acting. Translated, with Annotations, from Diderot's "Le Paradoxe sur le Comédien," by WALTER HERRIES POLLOCK. With a Preface by HENRY IRVING. Cr. 8vo, in parchment, 4s. 6d.

8   BOOKS PUBLISHED BY

Dobson (Austin). — Thomas Bewick and his Pupils. By AUSTIN DOBSON. With 95 ch ice Illustrations. Square 8vo, cloth extra, 6s.

Dobson (W. T.), Works by:
Post 8vo, cloth limp, 2s. 6d. each.
Literary Frivolities, Fancies, Follies, and Frolics.
Poetical Ingenuities and Eccentricities.

Donovan (Dick), Detective Stories by:
Post 8vo, illustrated boards, 2s. each; cloth limp, 2s. 6d. each.
The Man-hunter: Stories from the Note-book of a Detective.
Caught at Last!
Tracked and Taken.

Drama, A Dictionary of the.
Being a comprehensive Guide to the Plays, Playwrights, Players, and Playhouses of the United Kingdom and America, from the Earliest to the Present Times. By W. DAVENPORT ADAMS. (Uniform with BREWER'S "Reader's Handbook.") Crown 8vo, half-bound, 12s. 6d. [*In preparation.*

Dramatists, The Old. Cr. 8vo, cl. ex., Vignette Portraits, 6s. per Vol.
Ben Jonson's Works. With Notes Critical and Explanatory, and a Biographical Memoir by WM. GIFFORD. Edit. by Col. CUNNINGHAM. 3 Vols.
Chapman's Works. Complete in Three Vols. Vol. I. contains the Plays complete, including doubtful ones; Vol. II., Poems and Minor Translations, with Introductory Essay by A. C. SWINBURNE; Vol. III., Translations of the Iliad and Odyssey.
Marlowe's Works. Including his Translations. Edited, with Notes and Introduction, by Col. CUNNINGHAM. One Vol.
Massinger's Plays. From the Text of WILLIAM GIFFORD. Edited by Col. CUNNINGHAM. One Vol.

Dyer. — The Folk-Lore of Plants. By Rev. T. F. THISELTON DYER, M.A. Cr. 8vo, cloth extra, 6s.

Edgcumbe. — Zephyrus: A Holiday in Brazil and on the River Plate. By E. R. PEARCE EDGCUMBE. With 41 Illusts. Cr. 8vo, cl. extra, 5s.

Edwards.—Words, Facts, and Phrases: A Dictionary of Curious, Quaint, and Out-of-the-Way Matters. By ELIEZER EDWARDS. Crown 8vo, cloth extra, 7s. 6d.

Early English Poets. Edited, with Introductions and Annotations, by Rev. A. B. GROSART, D.D. Crown 8vo, cloth boards, 6s. per Volume.
Fletcher's (Giles, B.D.) Complete Poems. One Vol.
Davies' (Sir John) Complete Poetical Works. Two Vols.
Herrick's (Robert) Complete Collected Poems. Three Vols.
Sidney's (Sir Philip) Complete Poetical Works. Three Vols.

Edwardes (Mrs. A.), Novels by:
A Point of Honour. Post 8vo, illustrated boards, 2s.
Archie Lovell. Crown 8vo, cloth extra, 3s. 6d.; post 8vo, illust. bds., 2s.

Eggleston.—Roxy: A Novel. By EDWARD EGGLESTON. Post 8vo, illust. boards, 2s.

Emanuel.—On Diamonds and Precious Stones: their History, Value, and Properties; with Simple Tests for ascertaining their Reality. By HARRY EMANUEL, F.R.G.S. With numerous Illustrations, tinted and plain. Crown 8vo, cloth extra, 6s.

Englishman's House, The: A Practical Guide to all interested in Selecting or Building a House; with full Estimates of Cost, Quantities, &c. By C. J. RICHARDSON. Fourth Edition. With Coloured Frontispiece and nearly 600 Illustrations. Crown 8vo, cloth extra, 7s. 6d.

Ewald (Alex. Charles, F.S.A.), Works by:
The Life and Times of Prince Charles Stuart, Count of Albany, commonly called the Young Pretender. From the State Papers and other Sources. New and Cheaper Edition, with a Portrait. Crown 8vo, cloth extra, 7s. 6d.
Stories from the State Papers. With an Autotype Facsimile. Crown 8vo, cloth extra, 6s.

Eyes, Our: How to Preserve Them from Infancy to Old Age. By JOHN BROWNING, F.R.A.S., &c. Eighth Edition (Fourteenth Thousand). With 70 Illustrations. Crown 8vo, cloth, 1s.

Familiar Short Sayings of Great Men. By SAMUEL ARTHUR BENT, A.M. Fifth Edition, Revised and Enlarged. Cr. 8vo, cl. ex., 7s. 6d.

Farrer (J. Anson), Works by:
Military Manners and Customs. Crown 8vo, cloth extra, 6s.
War: Three Essays, Reprinted from "Military Manners." Crown 8vo, 1s.; cloth, 1s. 6d.

Faraday (Michael), Works by:
Post 8vo, cloth extra, 4s. 6d. each.
The Chemical History of a Candle:
Lectures delivered before a Juvenile Audience at the Royal Institution. Edited by WILLIAM CROOKES, F.C.S. With numerous Illustrations.
On the Various Forces of Nature, and their Relations to each other: Lectures delivered before a Juvenile Audience at the Royal Institution. Edited by WILLIAM CROOKES, F.C.S. With numerous Illustrations.

Fin-Bec.—The Cupboard Papers: Observations on the Art of Living and Dining. By FIN-BEC. Post 8vo, cloth limp, 2s. 6d.

Fireworks, The Complete Art of Making; or, The Pyrotechnist's Treasury. By THOMAS KENTISH. With 267 Illustrations. A New Edition, Revised throughout and greatly Enlarged. Crown 8vo, cloth extra, 5s.

Fitzgerald (Percy), Works by:
The World Behind the Scenes. Crown 8vo, cloth extra, 3s. 6d.
Little Essays: Passages from the Letters of CHARLES LAMB. Post 8vo, cloth limp, 2s. 6d.
A Day's Tour: A Journey through France and Belgium. With Sketches in facsimile of the Original Drawings. Crown 4to picture cover, 1s.
Fatal Zero: A Homburg Diary. Cr. 8vo, cloth extra, 3s. 6d.; post 8vo, illustrated boards, 2s.

Post 8vo, illustrated boards, 2s. each.
Bella Donna. | Never Forgotten.
The Second Mrs. Tillotson.
Seventy-five Brooke Street
Polly. | The Lady of Brantome.

Fletcher's (Giles, B.D.) Complete Poems: Christ's Victorie in Heaven, Christ's Victorie on Earth, Christ's Triumph over Death, and Minor Poems. With Memorial-Introduction and Notes by the Rev. A. B. GROSART, D.D. Cr. 8vo, cloth bds., 6s.

Fonblanque.—Filthy Lucre: A Novel. By ALBANY DE FONBLANQUE. Post 8vo, illustrated boards, 2s.

Frederic (Harold), Novels by:
Seth's Brother's Wife. Post 8vo, illustrated boards, 2s.
The Lawton Girl. With a Frontispiece by F. BARNARD. Crown 8vo, cloth extra, 6s. [Shortly.

French Literature, History of.
By HENRY VAN LAUN. Complete in 3 Vols., demy 8vo, cl. bds., 7s. 6d. each.

Francillon (R. E.), Novels by:
Crown 8vo, cloth extra, 3s. 6d. each; post 8vo, illust. boards, 2s. each.
One by One. | A Real Queen.
Queen Cophetua. | King or Knave?
Olympia. Post 8vo, illust. boards, 2s.
Esther's Glove. Fcap. 8vo, 1s.
Romances of the Law. With a Frontispiece by D. H. FRISTON. Crown 8vo, cloth extra, 6s.; post 8vo, illustrated boards, 2s.

Frenzeny.—Fifty Years on the Trail: The Adventures of JOHN Y. NELSON, Scout, Guide, and Interpreter, in the Wild West. By HARRINGTON O'REILLY. With over 100 Illustrations by PAUL FRENZENY. Crown 8vo, picture cover, 3s. 6d.; cloth extra, 4s. 6d.

Frere.—Pandurang Hari; or, Memoirs of a Hindoo. With a Preface by Sir H. BARTLE FRERE, G.C.S.I., &c. Crown 8vo, cloth extra, 3s. 6d.

Friswell.—One of Two: A Novel. By HAIN FRISWELL. Post 8vo, illustrated boards, 2s.

Frost (Thomas), Works by:
Crown 8vo, cloth extra, 3s. 6d. each.
Circus Life and Circus Celebrities.
The Lives of the Conjurers.
Old Showmen and Old London Fairs.

Fry's (Herbert) Royal Guide to the London Charities. Showing their Name, Date of Foundation, Objects, Income, Officials, &c. Edited by JOHN LANE. Published Annually. Crown 8vo, cloth, 1s. 6d.

Gardening Books:
Post 8vo, 1s. each; cl. limp, 1s. 6d. each.
A Year's Work in Garden and Greenhouse: Practical Advice to Amateur Gardeners as to the Management of the Flower, Fruit, and Frame Garden. By GEORGE GLENNY.
Our Kitchen Garden: The Plants we Grow, and How we Cook Them. By TOM JERROLD.
Household Horticulture: A Gossip about Flowers. By TOM and JANE JERROLD. Illustrated.
The Garden that Paid the Rent. By TOM JERROLD.

My Garden Wild, and What I Grew there. By F. G. HEATH. Crown 8vo, cloth extra, 5s.; gilt edges, 6s.

Garrett.—The Capel Girls: A Novel. By EDWARD GARRETT. Cr. 8vo, cl. ex., 3s. 6d.; post 8vo, illust. bds., 2s.

BOOKS PUBLISHED BY

Gentleman's Magazine (The) for 1880.—1s. Monthly.—In addition to the Articles upon subjects in Literature, Science, and Art, for which this Magazine has so high a reputation, "Table Talk" by SYLVANUS URBAN appears monthly.

** *Bound Volumes for recent years are kept in stock, cloth extra, price 8s. 6d. each; Cases for binding, 2s. each.*

Gentleman's Annual (The). Published Annually in November. In picture cover, demy 8vo, 1s.

German Popular Stories. Collected by the Brothers GRIMM, and Translated by EDGAR TAYLOR. Edited, with an Introduction, by JOHN RUSKIN. With 22 Illustrations on Steel by GEORGE CRUIKSHANK. Square 8vo, cloth extra, 6s. 6d.; gilt edges, 7s. 6d.

Gibbon (Charles), Novels by: Crown 8vo, cloth extra, 3s. 6d. each; post 8vo, illustrated boards, 2s. each.

Robin Gray.	The Braes of Yarrow.
What will the World Say?	A Heart's Problem.
Queen of the Meadow.	The Golden Shaft.
The Flower of the Forest.	Of High Degree.
	Loving a Dream.
In Honour Bound.	

Post 8vo, illustrated boards, 2s. each.
The Dead Heart.
For Lack of Gold.
For the King. | In Pastures Green.
In Love and War.
By Mead and Stream.
A Hard Knot. | Heart's Delight.
Blood-Money.

Gilbert (William), Novels by: Post 8vo, illustrated boards, 2s. each.
Dr. Austin's Guests.
The Wizard of the Mountain.
James Duke, Costermonger.

Gilbert (W. S.), Original Plays by: In Two Series, each complete in itself, price 2s. 6d. each.

The FIRST SERIES contains—The Wicked World—Pygmalion and Galatea—Charity—The Princess—The Palace of Truth—Trial by Jury.

The SECOND SERIES contains—Broken Hearts—Engaged—Sweethearts—Gretchen—Dan'l Druce—Tom Cobb—H.M.S. Pinafore—The Sorcerer—The Pirates of Penzance.

GILBERT (W. S.), *continued*—
Eight Original Comic Operas. Written by W. S. GILBERT. Containing: The Sorcerer—H.M.S. "Pinafore"—The Pirates of Penzance—Iolanthe —Patience — Princess Ida — The Mikado—Trial by Jury. Demy 8vo, cloth limp, 2s. 6d.

Glenny.—A Year's Work in Garden and Greenhouse: Practical Advice to Amateur Gardeners as to the Management of the Flower, Fruit, and Frame Garden. By GEORGE GLENNY. Post 8vo, 1s.; cloth, 1s. 6d.

Godwin.—Lives of the Necromancers. By WILLIAM GODWIN. Post 8vo, limp, 2s.

Golden Library, The: Square 16mo (Tauchnitz size), cloth limp, 2s. per Volume.
Bayard Taylor's Diversions of the Echo Club.
Bennett's (Dr. W. C.) Ballad History of England.
Bennett's (Dr.) Songs for Sailors.
Godwin's (William) Lives of the Necromancers.
Holmes's Autocrat of the Breakfast Table. Introduction by SALA.
Holmes's Professor at the Breakfast Table.
Hood's Whims and Oddities. Complete. All the original Illustrations.
Jesse's (Edward) Scenes and Occupations of a Country Life.
Leigh Hunt's Essays: A Tale for a Chimney Corner, and other Pieces. With Portrait, and an Introduction by EDMUND OLLIER.
Mallory's (Sir Thomas) Mort d'Arthur: The Stories of King Arthur and of the Knights of the Round Table. Edited by B. MONTGOMERIE RANKING.
Pascal's Provincial Letters. A New Translation, with Historical Introduction and Notes by T. M'CRIE, D.D.
Pope's Poetical Works.
Rochefoucauld's Maxims and Moral Reflections. With Notes, and Introductory Essay by SAINTE-BEUVE.

Golden Treasury of Thought, The: An ENCYCLOPÆDIA OF QUOTATIONS from Writers of all Times and Countries. Selected and Edited by THEODORE TAYLOR. Crown 8vo, cloth gilt and gilt edges, 7s. 6d.

Gowing. — Five Thousand Miles in a Sledge: A Mid-winter Journey Across Siberia. By LIONEL F. GOWING. With a Map by E. WELLER and 30 Illustrations by C. J. UREN, Large crown 8vo, cloth extra, 8s.

Graham. — The Professor's Wife: A Story. By LEONARD GRAHAM. Fcap. 8vo, picture cover, 1s.

Greeks and Romans, The Life of the, Described from Antique Monuments. By ERNST GUHL and W. KONER. Translated from the Third German Edition, and Edited by Dr. F. HUEFFER. With 545 Illustrations. New and Cheaper Edition, large crown 8vo, cloth extra, 7s. 6d.

Greenaway (Kate) and Bret Harte.—The Queen of the Pirate Isle. By BRET HARTE. With 25 original Drawings by KATE GREENAWAY, reproduced in Colours by E. EVANS. Sm. 4to, bds., 5s.

Greenwood (James), Works by: Crown 8vo, cloth extra, 3s. 6d. each.
The Wilds of London.
Low-Life Deeps: An Account of the Strange Fish to be Found There.

Greville (Henry), Novels by:
Nikanor: A Russian Novel. Translated by ELIZA E. CHASE. With 8 Illusts. Crown 8vo, cloth extra, 6s.
A Noble Woman. Translated by ALBERT D. VANDAM. Crown 8vo, cloth extra, 5s.

Habberton (John), Author of "Helen's Babies," Novels by:
Post 8vo, illustrated boards, 2s. each; cloth limp, 2s. 6d. each.
Brueton's Bayou.
Country Luck.

Hair (The): Its Treatment in Health, Weakness, and Disease. Translated from the German of Dr. J. PINCUS. Crown 8vo, 1s.; cloth, 1s. 6d.

Hake (Dr. Thomas Gordon), Poems by:
Crown 8vo, cloth extra, 6s. each.
New Symbols.
Legends of the Morrow.
The Serpent Play.
Maiden Ecstasy. Small 4to, cloth extra, 8s.

Hall.—Sketches of Irish Character. By Mrs. S. C. HALL. With numerous Illustrations on Steel and Wood by MACLISE, GILBERT, HARVEY, and G. CRUIKSHANK. Medium 8vo, cloth extra, 7s. 6d.

Halliday.—Every-day Papers. By ANDREW HALLIDAY. Post 8vo, illustrated boards, 2s.

Handwriting, The Philosophy of. With over 100 Facsimiles and Explanatory Text. By DON FELIX DE SALAMANCA. Post 8vo, cl. limp, 2s. 6d.

Hanky-Panky: A Collection of Very Easy Tricks, Very Difficult Tricks, White Magic, Sleight of Hand, &c. Edited by W. H. CREMER. With 200 Illusts. Crown 8vo, cloth extra, 4s. 6d.

Hardy (Lady Duffus). — Paul Wynter's Sacrifice: A Story. By Lady DUFFUS HARDY. Post 8vo, illustrated boards, 2s.

Hardy (Thomas).—Under the Greenwood Tree. By THOMAS HARDY, Author of "Far from the Madding Crowd." Post 8vo, illustrated bds., 2s.

Harwood.—The Tenth Earl. By J. BERWICK HARWOOD. Post 8vo, illustrated boards, 2s.

Haweis (Mrs. H. R.), Works by:
Square 8vo, cloth extra, 6s. each.
The Art of Beauty. With Coloured Frontispiece and numerous Illusts.
The Art of Decoration. With numerous Illustrations.
Chaucer for Children: A Golden Key. With Eight Coloured Pictures and numerous Woodcuts.
The Art of Dress. With numerous Illustrations. Small 8vo, illustrated cover, 1s.; cloth limp, 1s. 6d.
Chaucer for Schools. Demy 8vo, cloth limp, 2s. 6d.

Haweis (Rev. H. R.).—American Humorists: WASHINGTON IRVING, OLIVER WENDELL HOLMES, JAMES RUSSELL LOWELL, ARTEMUS WARD, MARK TWAIN, and BRET HARTE. By Rev. H. R. HAWEIS, M.A. Cr. 8vo, 6s.

Hawley Smart. — Without Love or Licence: A Novel. By HAWLEY SMART. Three Vols., crown 8vo. [Shortly.

Hawthorne (Julian), Novels by.
Crown 8vo, cloth extra, 3s. 6d. each;
post 8vo, illustrated boards, 2s. each.

Garth.	Sebastian Strome.
Ellice Quentin.	Dust.
Fortune's Fool.	Beatrix Randolph.

David Poindexter's Disappearance.
The Spectre of the Camera.
Post 8vo, illustrated boards, 2s. each.
Miss Cadogna. | Love—or a Name.
Mrs. Gainsborough's Diamonds. Fcap. 8vo, illustrated cover, 1s.
A Dream and a Forgetting. Post 8vo, cloth, 1s 6d.

Hays.—Women of the Day: A Biographical Dictionary of Notable Contemporaries. By FRANCES HAYS. Crown 8vo, cloth extra, 5s.

Heath (F. G.).—My Garden Wild, and What I Grew There. By FRANCIS GEORGE HEATH, Author of "The Fern World," &c. Crown 8vo, cloth extra, 5s.; cl. gilt, gilt edges, 6s.

Helps (Sir Arthur), Works by:
Post 8vo, cloth limp, 2s. 6d. each.
Animals and their Masters.
Social Pressure.

Ivan de Biron: A Novel. Crown 8vo, cloth extra, 3s. 6d.; post 8vo, illustrated boards, 2s.

Henderson.—Agatha Page: A Novel. By ISAAC HENDERSON. Crown 8vo, cloth extra, 3s. 6d.

Herrick's (Robert) Hesperides, Noble Numbers, and Complete Collected Poems. With Memorial-Introduction and Notes by the Rev. A. B. GROSART, D.D., Steel Portrait, Index of First Lines, and Glossarial Index, &c. Three Vols., crown 8vo, cloth, 18s.

Hesse-Wartegg (Chevalier Ernst von), Works by:
Tunis: The Land and the People. With 22 Illusts. Cr. 8vo, cl. ex., 3s. 6d.
The New South-West: Travelling Sketches from Kansas, New Mexico, Arizona, and Northern Mexico. With 100 fine Illustrations and Three Maps. Demy 8vo, cloth extra, 14s. [*In preparation.*

Hindley (Charles). Works by:
Tavern Anecdotes and Sayings: Including the Origin of Signs, and Reminiscences connected with Taverns, Coffee Houses, Clubs, &c. With Illustrations. Crown 8vo, cloth extra, 3s. 6d.
The Life and Adventures of a Cheap Jack. By One of the Fraternity. Edited by CHARLES HINDLEY. Crown 8vo, cloth extra, 3s. 6d.

Hoey.—The Lover's Creed. By Mrs. CASHEL HOEY. Post 8vo, illustrated boards, 2s.

Hollingshead—NiagaraSpray: Sketches. By JOHN HOLLINGSHEAD. Post 8vo, picture cover, 1s.

Holmes (O. Wendell), Works by:
The Autocrat of the Breakfast-Table. Illustrated by J. GORDON THOMSON. Post 8vo, cloth limp, 2s. 6d.—Another Edition in smaller type, with an Introduction by G. A. SALA. Post 8vo, cloth limp, 2s.
The Professor at the Breakfast-Table; with the Story of Iris. Post 8vo, cloth limp, 2s.

Holmes.—The Science of Voice Production and Voice Preservation: A Popular Manual for the Use of Speakers and Singers. By GORDON HOLMES, M.D. With Illustrations. Crown 8vo, 1s.; cloth, 1s. 6d.

Hood (Thomas):
Hood's Choice Works, in Prose and Verse. Including the Cream of the COMIC ANNUALS. With Life of the Author, Portrait, and 200 Illustrations. Crown 8vo, cloth extra, 7s. 6d.
Hood's Whims and Oddities. With all the original Illustrations. Post 8vo, cloth limp, 2s.

Hood (Tom).—From Nowhere to the North Pole: A Noah's Arkæological Narrative. By TOM HOOD. With 25 Illustrations by W. BRUNTON and E. C. BARNES. Square 8vo, cloth extra, gilt edges, 6s.

Hook's (Theodore) Choice Humorous Works, including his Ludicrous Adventures, Bons Mots, Puns, and Hoaxes. With Life of the Author, Portraits, Facsimiles, and Illustrations. Crown 8vo, cloth extra, 7s. 6d.

Hooper.—The House of Raby: A Novel. By Mrs. GEORGE HOOPER. Post 8vo, illustrated boards, 2s.

Hopkins—"'Twixt Love and Duty:" A Novel. By TIGHE HOPKINS. Post 8vo, illustrated boards, 2s.

Horne.—Orion: An Epic Poem, in Three Books. By RICHARD HENGIST HORNE. With Photographic Portrait from a Medallion by SUMMERS. Tenth Edition. Crown 8vo, cloth extra, 7s.

Horse (The) and his Rider: An Anecdotic Medley. By "THORMANBY." Crown 8vo, cloth extra, 6s.

Hunt.—Essays by Leigh Hunt: A Tale for a Chimney Corner, and other Piec s. With Portrait, and Introduction by EDMUND OLLIER. Post 8vo, cloth limp, 2s.

Hunt (Mrs. Alfred), Novels by:
Crown 8vo, cloth extra, 3s. 6d. each; post 8vo, illustrated boards, 2s. each.
Thornicroft's Model.
The Leaden Casket.
Self Condemned.
That other Person.

Hydrophobia: an Account of M. Pasteur's System. Containing a Translation of all his Communications on the Subject, the Technique of his Method, and the latest Statistical Results. By RENAUD SUZOR, M.B., C.M. Edin., and M.D. Paris, Commissioned by the Government of the Colony of Mauritius to study M. PASTEUR'S new Treatment in Paris. With 7 Illusts. Cr. 8vo, cloth extra, 6s.

Indoor Paupers. By ONE OF THEM. Crown 8vo, 1s.; cloth, 1s. 6d.

Ingelow.—Fated to be Free : A Novel. By JEAN INGELOW. Crown 8vo, cloth extra, 3s. 6d.; post 8vo, illustrated boards, 2s.

Irish Wit and Humour, Songs of. Collected and Edited by A. PERCEVALGRAVES. Post 8vo.cl.limp, 2s.6d.

James.—A Romance of the Queen's Hounds. By CHARLES JAMES. Post 8vo, picture cover, 1s.; cl., 1s. 6d.

Janvier.—Practical Keramics for Students. By CATHERINE A. JANVIER. Crown 8vo, cloth extra, 6s.

Jay (Harriett), Novels by:
Post 8vo, illustrated boards, 2s. each.
The Dark Colleen.
The Queen of Connaught.

Jefferies (Richard), Works by:
Nature near London. Crown 8vo, cl. ex., 6s.; post 8vo, cl. limp, 2s. 6d.
The Life of the Fields. Post 8vo, cloth limp, 2s. 6d.
The Open Air. Crown 8vo, cloth extra, 6s.; post 8vo, cl. limp, 2s. 6d.
The Eulogy of Richard Jefferies. By WALTER BESANT. Second Ed. Photo. Portrait. Cr. 8vo. cl. ex., 6s.

Jennings (H. J.), Works by:
Curiosities of Criticism. Post 8vo, cloth limp, 2s. 6d.
Lord Tennyson: A Biographical Sketch. With a Photograph-Portrait. Crown 8vo, cloth extra, 6s.

Jerome.—Stageland : Curious Habits and Customs of its Inhabitants. By JEROME K. JEROME, Author of " Idle Thoughts of an Idle Fellow." With 64 Illusts. by J. BERNARD PARTRIDGE. Fourth Edition. Fcap. 4to, cloth extra, 3s. 6d.

Jerrold (Tom), Works by :
Post 8vo, 1s. each; cloth, 1s. 6d. each.
The Garden that Paid the Rent.
Household Horticulture: A Gossip about Flowers. Illustrated.
Our Kitchen Garden: The Plants we Grow, and How we Cook Them.

Jesse.—Scenes and Occupations of a Country Life. By EDWARD JESSE. Post 8vo, cloth limp, 2s.

Jeux d'Esprit. Collected and Edited by HENRY S. LEIGH. Post 8vo, cloth limp, 2s. 6d.

Jones (Wm., F.S.A.), Works by:
Crown 8vo, cloth extra, 7s. 6d. each.
Finger-Ring Lore: Historical, Legendary, and Anecdotal. With over Two Hundred Illustrations.
Credulities, Past and Present. Including the Sea and Seamen, Miners, Talismans, Word and Letter Divination, Exorcising and Blessing of Animals, Birds, Eggs, Luck, &c. With an Etched Frontispiece.
Crowns and Coronations : A History of Regalia in all Times and Countries. One Hundred Illustrations

Jonson's (Ben) Works. With Notes Critical and Explanatory, and a Biographical Memoir by WILLIAM GIFFORD. Edited by Colonel CUNNINGHAM. Three Vols., crown 8vo, cloth extra, 18s.; or separately, 6s. each.

Josephus, The Complete Works of. Translated by WHISTON. Containing both "The Antiquities of the Jews" and "The Wars of the Jews." Two Vols., 8vo, with 52 Illustrations and Maps, cloth extra, gilt, 14s.

Kempt.—Pencil and Palette: Chapters on Art and Artists. By ROBERT KEMPT. Post 8vo, cloth limp, 2s. 6d.

Kershaw.—Colonial Facts and Fictions: Humorous Sketches. By MARK KERSHAW. Post 8vo, illustrated boards, 2s.; cloth, 2s. 6d.

Keyser.—Cut by the Mess: A Novel. By ARTHUR KEYSER. Cr. 8vo, picture cover, 1s.; cloth, 1s. 6d.

King (R. Ashe), Novels by:
Crown 8vo, cloth extra, 3s. 6d. each; post 8vo, illustrated boards, 2s. each.
A Drawn Game.
"The Wearing of the Green."
Passion's Slave. Three Vols. Crown 8vo.

Kingsley (Henry), Novels by:
Oakshott Castle. Post 8vo, illustrated boards, 2s.
Number Seventeen. Crown 8vo, cloth extra, 3s. 6d.

Knight.—The Patient's Vade Mecum: How to get most Benefit from Medical Advice. By WILLIAM KNIGHT, M.R.C.S., and EDW. KNIGHT, L.R.C.P. Cr. 8vo, 1s.; cloth, 1s. 6d.

BOOKS PUBLISHED BY

Knights (The) of the Lion: A Romance of the Thirteenth Century. Edited, with an Introduction, by the MARQUESS of LORNE, K.T. Crown 8vo cloth extra, 6s.

Lamb (Charles):
Lamb's Complete Works, in Prose and Verse, reprinted from the Original Editions, with many Pieces hitherto unpublished. Edited, with Notes and Introduction, by R. H. SHEPHERD. With Two Portraits and Facsimile of a page of the "Essay on Roast Pig." Cr. 8vo, cl. extra, 7s. 6d.
The Essays of Elia. Both Series complete. Post 8vo, laid paper, handsomely half-bound, 2s.
Poetry for Children, and Prince Dorus. By CHARLES LAMB. Carefully reprinted from unique copies. Small 8vo, cloth extra, 5s.
Little Essays: Sketches and Characters by CHARLES LAMB. Selected from his Letters by PERCY FITZGERALD. Post 8vo, cloth limp, 2s. 6d.

Lane's Arabian Nights.—The Thousand and One Nights: commonly called in England "THE ARABIAN NIGHTS' ENTERTAINMENTS." A New Translation from the Arabic, with copious Notes, by EDWARD WILLIAM LANE. Illustrated by many hundred Engravings on Wood, from Original Designs by WM. HARVEY. A New Edition, from a Copy annotated by the Translator, edited by his Nephew, EDWARD STANLEY POOLE. With a Preface by STANLEY LANE-POOLE. Three Vols., demy 8vo, cloth extra, 7s. 6d. each.

Larwood (Jacob), Works by:
The Story of the London Parks. With Illusts. Cr. 8vo, cl. ex., 3s. 6d.
Anecdotes of the Clergy: The Antiquities, Humours, and Eccentricities of the Cloth. Post 8vo, printed on laid paper and hf.-bound (uniform with "The Essays of Elia" and "Gastronomy as a Fine Art"), 2s.
Post 8vo, cloth limp, 2s. 6d. each.
Forensic Anecdotes.
Theatrical Anecdotes.

Leigh (Henry S.), Works by:
Carols of Cockayne. A New Edition, printed on fcap. 8vo hand-made paper, and bound in buckram, 5s.
Jeux d'Esprit. Collected and Edited by HENRY S. LEIGH. Post 8vo, cloth limp, 2s. 6d.

Leys.—The Lindsays: A Romance of Scottish Life. By JOHN K. LEYS. Post 8vo, illustrated boards, 2s.

Life in London; or, The History of Jerry Hawthorn and Corinthian Tom. With the whole of CRUIKSHANK'S Illustrations in Colours, after the Originals. Cr. 8vo, cl. extra, 7s. 6d.

Linskill.—In Exchange for a Soul. By MARY LINSKILL, Author of "The Haven Under the Hill," &c. Post 8vo, illustrated boards, 2s.

Linton (E. Lynn), Works by:
Post 8vo, cloth limp, 2s. 6d. each.
Witch Stories.
Ourselves: Essays on Women.
Crown 8vo, cloth extra, 3s. 6d. each; post 8vo, illustrated boards, 2s. each.
Patricia Kemball.
The Atonement of Leam Dundas.
The World Well Lost.
Under which Lord?
"My Love!" | Ione.
Paston Carew, Millionaire & Miser.
Post 8vo, illustrated boards, 2s. each.
With a Silken Thread.
The Rebel of the Family.

Longfellow's Poetical Works. Carefully Reprinted from the Original Editions. With numerous fine Illustrations on Steel and Wood. Crown 8vo, cloth extra, 7s. 6d.

Long Life, Aids to: A Medical, Dietetic, and General Guide in Health and Disease. By N. E. DAVIES, L.R.C.P. Cr. 8vo, 2s.; cl. limp, 2s.6d.

Lucy.—Gideon Fleyce: A Novel. By HENRY W. LUCY. Crown 8vo, cl. ex., 3s. 6d.; post 8vo, illust. bds., 2s.

Lusiad (The) of Camoens. Translated into English Spenserian Verse by ROBERT FFRENCH DUFF. Demy 8vo, with Fourteen full-page Plates, cloth boards, 18s.

Macalpine (Avery), Novels by:
Teresa Itasca, and other Stories. Crown 8vo, bound in canvas, 2s. 6d.
Broken Wings. With Illusts. by W. J. HENNESSY. Cr. 8vo, cloth extra, 6s.

McCarthy (Justin H., M.P.), Works by:
The French Revolution. 4 Vols., demy 8vo, 12s. each.
[Vols. I. & II. *in the press.*
An Outline of the History of Ireland, from the Earliest Times to the Present Day. Cr. 8vo, 1s.; cloth, 1s. 6d.
Ireland since the Union: Sketches of Irish History from 1798 to 1886. Crown 8vo, cloth extra, 6s.
England under Gladstone, 1880-85. Second Edition, revised. Crown 8vo, cloth extra, 6s.
Hafiz in London: Poems. Choicely printed. Small 8vo, gold cloth, 3s. 6d.

CHATTO & WINDUS, PICCADILLY. 15

McCarthy (Justin H.), continued—
Harlequinade: Poems. Small 4to, Japanese vellum, 8s.
Our Sensation Novel. Crown 8vo, 1s.; cloth, 1s. 6d.
Dolly: A Sketch. Crown 8vo, picture cover, 1s.; cloth, 1s. 6d.
Lily Lass: A Romance. Crown 8vo, picture cover, 1s.; cloth, 1s. 6d.

McCarthy (J., M.P.), Works by:
A History of Our Own Times, from the Accession of Queen Victoria to the General Election of 1880. Four Vols. demy 8vo, cloth extra, 12s. each.—Also a POPULAR EDITION, in Four Vols. cr. 8vo, cl. extra, 6s. each. —And a JUBILEE EDITION, with an Appendix of Events to the end of 1886, complete in Two Vols., square 8vo, cloth extra, 7s. 6d. each.
A Short History of Our Own Times. One Vol., crown 8vo, cloth extra, 6s. —Also a CHEAP POPULAR EDITION, in post 8vo, cloth extra, 2s. 6d.
A History of the Four Georges. Four Vols. demy 8vo, cloth extra, 12s. each.   [Vols. I. & II. *now ready*.

Crown 8vo, cloth extra, 3s. 6d. each; post 8vo, illustrated boards, 2s. each.
Dear Lady Disdain. | A Fair Saxon.
The Waterdale Neighbours.
Miss Misanthrope.
Donna Quixote. | Maid of Athens.
The Comet of a Season.
Camiola: A Girl with a Fortune.

Post 8vo, illustrated boards, 2s. each.
Linley Rochford.
My Enemy's Daughter.
"The Right Honourable:" A Romance of Society and Politics. By JUSTIN McCARTHY, M.P., and Mrs. CAMPBELL-PRAED. Cr. 8vo, cl. ex., 6s.

MacDonald.—Works of Fancy and Imagination. By GEORGE MACDONALD, LL.D. Ten Volumes, in handsome cloth case, 21s.—Vol. 1. WITHIN AND WITHOUT. THE HIDDEN LIFE.—Vol. 2. THE DISCIPLE. THE GOSPEL WOMEN. A BOOK OF SONNETS, ORGAN SONGS.—Vol. 3. VIOLIN SONGS. SONGS OF THE DAYS AND NIGHTS. A BOOK OF DREAMS. ROADSIDE POEMS. POEMS FOR CHILDREN. Vol. 4. PARABLES. BALLADS. SCOTCH SONGS.— Vols. 5 and 6. PHANTASTES: A Faerie Romance.—Vol. 7. THE PORTENT.— Vol. 8. THE LIGHT PRINCESS. THE GIANT'S HEART. SHADOWS.—Vol. 9. CROSS PURPOSES. THE GOLDEN KEY. THE CARASOYN. LITTLE DAYLIGHT.— Vol. 10. THE CRUEL PAINTER. THE WOW O' RIVVEN. THE CASTLE. THE BROKEN SWORDS. THE GRAY WOLF. UNCLE CORNELIUS.
The Volumes are also sold separately, in Grolier-pattern cloth, at 2s. 6d. each.

MacColl.—Mr. Stranger's Sealed Packet: A Story of Adventure. By HUGH MACCOLL. Second Edition. Crown 8vo, cloth extra, 5s.

Macdonell.—Quaker Cousins: A Novel. By AGNES MACDONELL. Crown 8vo, cloth extra, 3s. 6d.; post 8vo, illustrated boards, 2s.

Macgregor. — Pastimes and Players. Notes on Popular Games. By ROBERT MACGREGOR. Post 8vo, cloth limp, 2s. 6d.

Mackay.—Interludes and Undertones; or, Music at Twilight. By CHARLES MACKAY, LL.D. Crown 8vo, cloth extra, 6s.

Maclise Portrait-Gallery (The) of Illustrious Literary Characters; with Memoirs—Biographical, Critical, Bibliographical, and Anecdotal—illustrative of the Literature of the former half of the Present Century. By WILLIAM BATES, B.A. With 85 Portraits printed on an India Tint. Crown 8vo, cloth extra, 7s. 6d.

Macquoid (Mrs.), Works by:
Square 8vo, cloth extra, 7s. 6d. each.
In the Ardennes. With 50 fine Illustrations by THOMAS R. MACQUOID.
Pictures and Legends from Normandy and Brittany. With numerous Illusts. by THOMAS R. MACQUOID.
Through Normandy. With 90 Illustrations by T. R. MACQUOID.
Through Brittany. With numerous Illustrations by T. R. MACQUOID.
About Yorkshire. With 67 Illustrations by T. R. MACQUOID.

Post 8vo, illustrated boards, 2s. each.
The Evil Eye, and other Stories.
Lost Rose.

Magician's Own Book (The): Performances with Cups and Balls, Eggs, Hats, Handkerchiefs, &c. All from actual Experience. Edited by W. H. CREMER. With 200 Illustrations. Crown 8vo, cloth extra, 4s. 6d.

Magic Lantern (The), and its Management: including full Practical Directions for producing the Limelight, making Oxygen Gas, and preparing Lantern Slides. By T. C. HEPWORTH. With 10 Illustrations. Crown 8vo, 1s.; cloth, 1s. 6d.

Magna Charta. An exact Facsimile of the Original in the British Museum, printed on fine plate paper, 3 feet by 2 feet, with Arms and Seals emblazoned in Gold and Colours, 5s.

Mallock (W. H.), Works by:
The New Republic; or, Culture, Faith, and Philosophy in an English Country House. Post 8vo, picture cover, 2s.; cloth limp, 2s. 6d.
The New Paul and Virginia; or, Positivism on an Island. Post 8vo, cloth limp, 2s. 6d.
Poems. Small 4to, parchment, 8s.
Is Life worth Living? Crown 8vo, cloth extra, 6s.

Mallory's (Sir Thomas) Mort d'Arthur:
The Stories of King Arthur and o' the Knights of the Round Table. A Selection. Edited by B. MONTGOMERIE RANKING. Post 8vo, cloth limp, 2s.

Man-Hunter (The):
Stories from the Note-book of a Detective. By DICK DONOVAN. Post 8vo, illustrated boards, 2s.; cloth, 2s. 6d.

Mark Twain, Works by:
Crown 8vo, cloth extra, 7s. 6d. each.
The Choice Works of Mark Twain. Revised and Corrected throughout by the Author. With Life, Portrait, and numerous Illustrations.
Roughing It, and The Innocents at Home. With 200 Illustrations by F. A. FRASER.
The Gilded Age. By MARK TWAIN and CHARLES DUDLEY WARNER. With 212 Illustrations by T. COPPIN.
Mark Twain's Library of Humour. With numerous Illustrations.
A Yankee at the Court of King Arthur. With 220 Illustrations by DAN BEARD.

Crown 8vo, cloth extra, (illustrated), 7s. 6d. each; post 8vo (without Illustrations), illustrated boards, 2s. each.
The Innocents Abroad; or, The New Pilgrim's Progress: "MARK TWAIN'S PLEASURE TRIP."
The Adventures of Tom Sawyer. With 111 Illustrations.
The Prince and the Pauper. With nearly 200 Illustrations.
A Tramp Abroad. With 314 Illusts.
Life on the Mississippi. With 300 Illustrations.
The Adventures of Huckleberry Finn. With 174 Illustrations by E. W. KEMBLE.

The Stolen White Elephant, &c. Crown 8vo, cloth extra, 6s.; post 8vo, illustrated boards, 2s.

Marlowe's Works.
Including his Translations. Edited, with Notes and Introductions, by Col. CUNNINGHAM. Crown 8vo, cloth extra, 6s.

Marryat (Florence), Novels by:
Post 8vo, illustrated boards, 2s. each.
A Harvest of Wild Oats.
Fighting the Air. | Written in Fire.
Open! Sesame! Crown 8vo, cloth extra, 3s. 6d.; post 8vo, picture boards, 2s.

Massinger's Plays.
From the Text of WM. GIFFORD. Edited by Col. CUNNINGHAM. Cr. 8vo, cloth extra, 6s.

Masterman.—Half a Dozen
Daughters: A Novel. By J. MASTERMAN. Post 8vo, illustrated boards, 2s.

Matthews.—A Secret of the
Sea, &c. By BRANDER MATTHEWS. Post 8vo, illust. bds., 2s.; cloth, 2s. 6d.

Mayfair Library, The:
Post 8vo, cloth limp, 2s. 6d. per Volume.
A Journey Round My Room. By XAVIER DE MAISTRE. Translated by HENRY ATTWELL.
Quips and Quiddities. Selected by W. DAVENPORT ADAMS.
The Agony Column of "The Times," from 1800 to 1870. Edited, with an Introduction, by ALICE CLAY.
Melancholy Anatomised: A Popular Abridgment of "Burton's Anatomy of Melancholy."
The Speeches of Charles Dickens.
Literary Frivolities, Fancies, Follies, and Frolics. By W. T. DOBSON.
Poetical Ingenuities and Eccentricities. Selected and Edited by W. T. DOBSON.
The Cupboard Papers. By FIN-BEC.
Original Plays by W. S. GILBERT. FIRST SERIES. Containing: The Wicked World — Pygmalion and Galatea— Charity— The Princess— The Palace of Truth—Trial by Jury.
Original Plays by W. S GILBERT. SECOND SERIES. Containing: Broken Hearts — Engaged — Sweethearts — Gretchen—Dan'l Druce—Tom Cobb —H.M.S. Pinafore — The Sorcerer —The Pirates of Penzance.
Songs of Irish Wit and Humour. Collected and Edited by A. PERCEVAL GRAVES.
Animals and their Masters. By Sir ARTHUR HELPS.
Social Pressure. By Sir A. HELPS.
Curiosities of Criticism. By HENRY J. JENNINGS.
The Autocrat of the Breakfast-Table. By OLIVER WENDELL HOLMES. Illustrated by J. GORDON THOMSON.
Pencil and Palette. By R. KEMPT.
Little Essays: Sketches and Characters by CHAS. LAMB. Selected from his Letters by PERCY FITZGERALD.
Forensic Anecdotes; or, Humour and Curiosities of the Law and Men of Law. By JACOB LARWOOD.

CHATTO & WINDUS, PICCADILLY. 17

MAYFAIR LIBRARY, *continued*—
Post 8vo, cloth limp, **2s. 6d.** per Volume.
Theatrical Anecdotes. By JACOB LARWOOD.
Jeux d'Esprit. Edited by HENRY S. LEIGH.
Witch Stories. By E. LYNN LINTON.
Ourselves: Essays on Women. By E. LYNN LINTON.
Pastimes and Players. By ROBERT MACGREGOR.
The New Paul and Virginia. By W. H. MALLOCK.
New Republic. By W. H. MALLOCK.
Puck on Pegasus. By H. CHOLMONDELEY-PENNELL.
Pegasus Re-Saddled. By H. CHOLMONDELEY-PENNELL. Illustrated by GEORGE DU MAURIER.
Muses of Mayfair. Edited by H. CHOLMONDELEY-PENNELL.
Thoreau: His Life and Aims. By H. A. PAGE.
Puniana. By the Hon. HUGH ROWLEY.
More Puniana. By Hon. H. ROWLEY.
The Philosophy of Handwriting. By DON FELIX DE SALAMANCA.
By Stream and Sea By WILLIAM SENIOR.
Leaves from a Naturalist's Note-Book. By Dr. ANDREW WILSON.

Mayhew.—London Characters and the Humorous Side of London Life. By HENRY MAYHEW. With numerous Illusts. Cr. 8vo, cl. extra, **3s. 6d.**

Medicine, Family.—One Thousand Medical Maxims and Surgical Hints, for Infancy, Adult Life, Middle Age, and Old Age. By N. E. DAVIES, L.R.C.P. Lond. Cr. 8vo, **1s.**; cl., **1s. 6d.**

Menken.—Infelicia: Poems by ADAH ISAACS MENKEN. A New Edition, with a Biographical Preface, numerous Illustrations by F. E. LUMMIS and F. O. C. DARLEY, and Facsimile of a Letter from CHARLES DICKENS. Beautifully printed on small 4to ivory paper, with red border to each page, and handsomely bound, price **7s. 6d.**

Mexican Mustang (On a), through Texas, from the Gulf to the Rio Grande. By A. E. SWEET and J. ARMOY KNOX, Editors of "Texas Siftings." With 265 Illusts. Cr. 8vo, cl. extra, **7s. 6d.**

Middlemass (Jean), Novels by:
Post 8vo, illustrated boards. **2s.** each.
Touch and Go. | Mr. Dorillion.

Miller.—**Physiology for the Young**; or, The House of Life: Human Physiology, with its application to the Preservation of Health. With numerous Illusts. By Mrs. F. FENWICK MILLER. Small 8vo, cloth limp, **2s. 6d.**

Milton (J. L.), Works by:
Sm. 8vo, **1s.** each; cloth ex., **1s. 6d.** each.
The Hygiene of the Skin. Rules for the Management of the Skin; with Directions for Diet, Soaps, Baths, &c.
The Bath in Diseases of the Skin.
The Laws of Life, and their Relation to Diseases of the Skin.

Minto.—Was She Good or Bad? A Romance. By WILLIAM MINTO. Cr. 8vo, picture cover, **1s.**; cloth, **1s. 6d.**

Molesworth (Mrs.), Novels by:
Hathercourt Rectory. Post 8vo, illustrated boards, **2s.**
That Girl in Black. Crown 8vo, picture cover, **1s.**; cloth, **1s. 6d.**

Moore (Thomas), Works by:
The Epicurean, and Alciphron. A New Edition. Post 8vo, printed on laid paper and half-bound, **2s.**
Prose and Verse, Humorous, Satirical, and Sentimental, by T. MOORE; with Suppressed Passages from the Memoirs of Lord Byron. Edited, with Notes and Introduction, by R. HERNE SHEPHERD. With Portrait. Crown 8vo, cloth extra, **7s. 6d.**

Muddock (J. E.), Stories by:
Stories Weird and Wonderful. Post 8vo, illust. boards, **2s.**; cloth, **2s. 6d.**
The Dead Man's Secret; or, The Valley of Gold: Being a Narrative of Strange and Wild Adventure. With a Frontispiece by F. BARNARD. Crown 8vo, cloth extra, **5s.**
The Man from Manchester. With a Frontispiece. Crown 8vo, cloth extra, **6s.** [*Shortly.*

Murray (D. Christie), Novels by. Crown 8vo, cloth extra, **3s. 6d.** each; post 8vo, illustrated boards, **2s.** each.
A Life's Atonement. | A Model Father.
Joseph's Coat. | Coals of Fire.
By the Gate of the Sea.| Hearts.
Val Strange. | Cynic Fortune.
A Bit of Human Nature.
First Person Singular.
The Way of the World.

Old Blazer's Hero. With Three Illustrations by A. McCORMICK. Crown 8vo, cloth extra, **6s.**; post 8vo, illustrated boards, **2s.**

Murray (D. Christie) & Henry Herman, Works by:
One Traveller Returns. Cr. 8vo, cloth extra, **6s.**; post 8vo, illust. bds., **2s.**
Paul Jones's Alias, &c. With Illusts. by A. FORESTIER and G. NICOLET. Crown 8vo, cloth extra, **6s.** [*Shortly.*
The Bishop's Bible. Three Vols., crown 8vo. [*Shortly.*

Murray.—A Game of Bluff: A Novel. By HENRY MURRAY, joint-Author with CHRISTIE MURRAY of " A Dangerous Catspaw." Post 8vo, picture boards, 2s.; cloth, 2s. 6d.

Novelists.— Half-Hours with the Best Novelists of the Century: Choice Readings from the finest Novels. Edited, with Critical and Biographical Notes, by H. T. MACKENZIE BELL. Crown 8vo, cl. ex., 3s. 6d. [*Preparing.*

Nursery Hints: A Mother's Guide in Health and Disease. By N. E. DAVIES, L.R.C.P. Cr.8vo, 1s.; cl., 1s.6d.

Oberammergau.—The Country of the Passion Play, and the Highlands of Bavaria. By L. G. SEGUIN, Author of " Walks in Algiers." With a Map and 37 Illustrations. Third Edition, with a new Preface for 1890. Cr. 8vo, cloth extra, 3s. 6d.

O'Connor.—Lord Beaconsfield: A Biography. By T. P. O'CONNOR, M.P. Sixth Edition, with a New Preface. Crown 8vo, cloth extra, 5s.

O'Hanlon (Alice), Novels by:
Post 8vo, illustrated boards, 2s. each.
The Unforeseen.
Chance? or Fate?

Ohnet (Georges), Novels by:
Doctor Rameau. Translated by Mrs. CASHEL HOEY. With 9 Illustrations by E. BAYARD. Cr. 8vo, cloth extra, 6s.; post 8vo, illustrated boards, 2s.
A Last Love. Translated by ALBERT D. VANDAM. Crown 8vo, cl. ex., 5s.

Oliphant (Mrs.), Novels by:
Whiteladies. With Illustrations by ARTHUR HOPKINS and H. WOODS. Crown 8vo, cloth extra, 3s. 6d.; post 8vo, illustrated boards, 2s.

Post 8vo, illustrated boards, 2s. each.
The Primrose Path.
The Greatest Heiress in England.

O'Reilly.—Phœbe's Fortunes: A Novel. With Illustrations by HENRY TUCK. Post 8vo, illustrated boards, 2s.

O'Shaughnessy (A.), Poems by:
Songs of a Worker. Fcap. 8vo, cloth extra, 7s. 6d.
Music and Moonlight. Fcap. 8vo, cloth extra, 7s. 6d.
Lays of France. Cr.8vo, cl. ex.,10s. 6d.

Ouida, Novels by. Crown 8vo, cloth extra, 3s. 6d. each; post 8vo, illustrated boards, 2s. each.

Held In Bondage.	Pascarel.
Strathmore.	Signa. | Ariadne.
Chandos	In a Winter City.
Under Two Flags.	Friendship.
Cecil Castle-	Moths. | Bimbi.
maine's Gage.	Pipistrello.
Idalia.	In Maremma
Tricotrin.	A Village Com-
Puck.	mune.
Folle Farine.	Wanda.
Two Little Wooden	Frescoes. [Ine.
Shoes.	Princess Naprax-
A Dog of Flanders.	Othmar.

Guilderoy. Crown 8vo, cloth extra, 3s. 6d.
Position. Three Vols., crown 8vo.

Wisdom, Wit, and Pathos, selected from the Works of OUIDA by F. SYDNEY MORRIS. Sm.cr.8vo,cl.,limp,5s.
CHEAPER EDITION, illust. bds., 2s.

Page (H. A.), Works by:
Thoreau His Life and Aims: A Study. With Portrait. Post 8vo,cl.limp,2s.6d.
Lights on the Way: Some Tales within a Tale. By the late J. H. ALEX-ANDER, B.A. Edited by H. A. PAGE. Crown 8vo, cloth extra, 6s.
Animal Anecdotes. Arranged on a New Principle. Cr. 8vo, cl. extra, 5s.

Parliamentary Elections and Electioneering in the Old Days (A History of). Showing the State of Political Parties and Party Warfare at the Hustings and in the House of Commons from the Stuarts to Queen Victoria. Illustrated from the original Political Squibs, Lampoons, Pictorial Satires, and Popular Caricatures of the Time. By JOSEPH GREGO, Author of "Rowlandson and his Works," "The Life of Gillray," &c. A New Edition, crown 8vo, cloth extra, with Coloured Frontispiece and 100 Illustrations, 7s. 6d. [*Preparing.*

Pascal's Provincial Letters. A New Translation, with Historical Introduction and Notes, by T. M'CRIE, D.D. Post 8vo, cloth limp, 2s.

Patient's (The) Vade Mecum: How to get most Benefit from Medical Advice. By W. KNIGHT, M.R.C.S., and E.KNIGHT, L.R.C.P. Cr.8vo, 1s.; cl. 1/6.

Paul Ferroll: why he Killed his Wife. Post 8vo, illustrated boards, 2s.

Paul.—Gentle and Simple. By MARGARET AGNES PAUL. With a Frontispiece by HELEN PATERSON. Cr. 8vo, cloth extra, 3s. 6d. ; post 8vo, illustrated boards, 2s.

Payn (James), Novels by.
Crown 8vo, cloth extra, 3s. 6d. each; post 8vo, illustrated boards, 2s. each.
Lost Sir Massingberd.
Walter's Word.
Less Black than we're Painted.
By Proxy. | High Spirits.
Under One Roof.
A Confidential Agent.
Some Private Views.
A Grape from a Thorn.
The Talk of the Town.
From Exile. | The Canon's Ward
Holiday Tasks. | Glow-worm Tales.
The Mystery of Mirbridge.

Post 8vo, illustrated boards, 2s. each.
Kit: A Memory. | Carlyon's Year.
A Perfect Treasure.
Bentinck's Tutor.|Murphy's Master.
The Best of Husbands.
For Cash Only.
What He Cost Her.| Cecil's Tryst.
Fallen Fortunes. | Halves.
A County Family. | At Her Mercy.
A Woman's Vengeance.
The Clyffards of Clyffe.
The Family Scapegrace.
The Foster Brothers.| Found Dead.
Gwendoline's Harvest.
Humorous Stories.
Like Father, Like Son.
A Marine Residence.
Married Beneath Him.
Mirk Abbey. | Not Wooed, but Won.
Two Hundred Pounds Reward.

In Peril and Privation: Stories of Marine Adventure Re-told. With 17 Illustrations. Crown 8vo, cloth extra, 3s. 6d.
The Burnt Million. Three Vols., crown 8vo.   [*Shortly*.

Pears.—The Present Depression in Trade: Its Causes and Remedies. Being the "Pears" Prize Essays (of One Hundred Guineas). By EDWIN GOADBY and WILLIAM WATT. With an Introductory Paper by Prof. LEONE LEVI, F.S.A., F.S.S. Demy 8vo, 1s.

Pennell (H. Cholmondeley), Works by:
Post 8vo, cloth limp, 2s. 6d. each.
Puck on Pegasus. With Illustrations.
Pegasus Re-Saddled. With Ten full-page Illusts. by G. DU MAURIER.
The Muses of Mayfair. Vers de Société, Selected and Edited by H. C. PENNELL.

Phelps (E. Stuart), Works by:
Post 8vo, 1s. each ; cl. limp, 1s. 6d. each.
Beyond the Gates. By the Author of "The Gates Ajar."
An Old Maid's Paradise.
Burglars in Paradise.

Jack the Fisherman. With Twenty-two Illustrations by C. W. REED. Cr. 8vo, picture cover, 1s. ; cl. 1s. 6d.

Pirkis (C. L.), Novels by:
Trooping with Crows. Fcap. 8vo, picture cover, 1s.
Lady Lovelace. Post 8vo, illustrated boards, 2s.

Planché (J. R.), Works by:
The Pursuivant of Arms ; or, Heraldry Founded upon Facts. With Coloured Frontispiece and 200 Illustrations. Cr. 8vo, cloth extra, 7s. 6d.
Songs and Poems, from 1819 to 1879. Edited, with an Introduction, by his Daughter, Mrs. MACKARNESS. Crown 8vo, cloth extra, 6s.

Plutarch's Lives of Illustrious Men. Translated from the Greek, with Notes Critical and Historical, and a Life of Plutarch, by JOHN and WILLIAM LANGHORNE. Two Vols., 8vo, cloth extra, with Portraits, 10s. 6d.

Poe (Edgar Allan):
The Choice Works, in Prose and Poetry, of EDGAR ALLAN POE. With an Introductory Essay by CHARLES BAUDELAIRE, Portrait and Facsimiles. Crown 8vo, cloth extra, 7s. 6d.
The Mystery of Marie Roget, and other Stories. Post 8vo, illust.bds.,2s.

Pope's Poetical Works. Complete in One Vol. Post 8vo, cl. limp, 2s.

Praed (Mrs. Campbell-).—"The Right Honourable:" A Romance of Society and Politics. By Mrs. CAMPBELL-PRAED and JUSTIN MCCARTHY, M.P. Crown 8vo, cloth extra, 6s.

Price (E. C.), Novels by:
Crown 8vo, cloth extra, 3s. 6d. each ; post 8vo, illustrated boards, 2s. each.
Valentina. | The Foreigners.
Mrs. Lancaster's Rival.

Gerald. Post 8vo, illust. boards, 2s.

Princess Olga—Radna; or, The Great Conspiracy of 1881. By the Princess OLGA. Cr. 8vo, cl. ex., 6s.

Proctor (R. A.), Works by:

Flowers of the Sky. With 55 Illusts. Small crown 8vo, cloth extra, 3s. 6d.
Easy Star Lessons. With Star Maps for Every Night in the Year, Drawings of the Constellations, &c. Crown 8vo, cloth extra, 6s.
Familiar Science Studies. Crown 8vo, cloth extra, 6s.
Saturn and its System. New and Revised Edition, with 13 Steel Plates. Demy 8vo, cloth extra, 10s. 6d.
Mysteries of Time and Space. With Illusts. Cr. 8vo, cloth extra, 6s.
The Universe of Suns, and other Science Gleanings. With numerous Illusts. Cr. 8vo, cloth extra, 6s.
Wages and Wants of Science Workers. Crown 8vo, 1s. 6d.

Rambosson.—Popular Astronomy. By J. RAMBOSSON, Laureate of the Institute of France. Translated by C. B. PITMAN. With numerous Illustrations and a Coloured Chart of Spectra. Crown 8vo, cloth extra, 7s. 6d.

Reade (Charles), Novels by:

Crown 8vo, cloth extra, illustrated, 3s. 6d. each; post 8vo, illust. bds., 2s. each.
Peg Woffington. Illustrated by S. L. FILDES, A.R.A.
Christie Johnstone. Illustrated by WILLIAM SMALL.
It is Never Too Late to Mend. Illustrated by G. J. PINWELL.
The Course of True Love Never did run Smooth. Illustrated by HELEN PATERSON.
The Autobiography of a Thief; Jack of all Trades; and James Lambert. Illustrated by MATT STRETCH.
Love me Little, Love me Long. Illustrated by M. ELLEN EDWARDS.
The Double Marriage. Illust. by Sir JOHN GILBERT, R.A., and C. KEENE.
The Cloister and the Hearth. Illustrated by CHARLES KEENE.
Hard Cash. Illust. by F. W. LAWSON.
Griffith Gaunt. Illustrated by S. L. FILDES, A.R.A., and WM. SMALL.
Foul Play. Illust. by Du MAURIER.
Put Yourself in His Place. Illustrated by ROBERT BARNES.
A Terrible Temptation. Illustrated by EDW. HUGHES and A. W. COOPER.
The Wandering Heir. Illustrated by H. PATERSON, S. L. FILDES, A.R.A., C. GREEN, and H. WOODS, A.R.A.
A Simpleton. Illustrated by KATE CRAUFORD. [COULDERY.
A Woman-Hater. Illust. by THOS.
Singleheart and Doubleface: A Matter-of-fact Romance. Illustrated by P. MACNAB.

READE (CHARLES), continued—
Good Stories of Men and other Animals. Illustrated by E. A. ABBEY, PERCY MACQUOID, and JOSEPH NASH.
The Jilt, and other Stories. Illustrated by JOSEPH NASH.
Readiana. With a Steel-plate Portrait of CHARLES READE.

Bible Characters: Studies of David, Nehemiah, Jonah, Paul, &c. Fcap. 8vo, leatherette, 1s.

Reader's Handbook (The) of Allusions, References, Plots, and Stories. By the Rev. Dr. BREWER. With an Appendix, containing a COMPLETE ENGLISH BIBLIOGRAPHY. Fifteenth Thousand. Crown 8vo, 1,400 pages, cloth extra, 7s. 6d.

Riddell (Mrs. J. H.), Novels by:

Crown 8vo, cloth extra, 3s. 6d. each; post 8vo, illustrated boards, 2s. each.
Her Mother's Darling.
The Prince of Wales's Garden Party.
Weird Stories.

Post 8vo, illustrated boards, 2s. each.
The Uninhabited House.
Fairy Water.
The Mystery in Palace Gardens.

Rimmer (Alfred), Works by:

Square 8vo, cloth gilt, 7s. 6d. each.
Our Old Country Towns. With over 50 Illustrations.
Rambles Round Eton and Harrow. With 50 Illustrations.
About England with Dickens. With 58 Illustrations by ALFRED RIMMER and C. A. VANDERHOOF.

Robinson Crusoe. By DANIEL DEFOE. (MAJOR'S EDITION.) With 37 Woodcut Illustrations by GEORGE CRUIKSHANK. Post 8vo, handsomely half-bound (uniform with Lamb's "Elia"), 2s. [Shortly.

Robinson (F. W.), Novels by:

Crown 8vo, cloth extra, 3s. 6d. each; post 8vo, illustrated boards, 2s. each.
Women are Strange.
The Hands of Justice.

Robinson (Phil), Works by:

Crown 8vo, cloth extra, 7s. 6d. each.
The Poets' Birds.
The Poets' Beasts.
The Poets and Nature: Reptiles, Fishes, and Insects. [Preparing.

Rochefoucauld's Maxims and Moral Reflections. With Notes, and an Introductory Essay by SAINTE-BEUVE. Post 8vo, cloth limp, 2s.

CHATTO & WINDUS, PICCADILLY.

Roll of Battle Abbey, The; or, A List of the Principal Warriors who came over from Normandy with William the Conqueror, and Settled in this Country, A.D. 1066-7. With the principal Arms emblazoned in Gold and Colours. Handsomely printed, 5s.

Rowley (Hon. Hugh), Works by:
Post 8vo, cloth limp, 2s. 6d. each.
Puniana: Riddles and Jokes. With numerous Illustrations.
More Puniana. Profusely Illustrated.

Runciman (James), Stories by:
Post 8vo, illustrated boards, 2s. each; cloth limp, 2s. 6d. each.
Skippers and Shellbacks.
Grace Balmaign's Sweetheart.
Schools and Scholars.

Russell (W. Clark), Works by:
Crown 8vo, cloth extra, 6s. each; post 8vo, illustrated boards, 2s. each.
Round the Galley-Fire.
In the Middle Watch.
A Voyage to the Cape.
A Book for the Hammock.
The Mystery of the "Ocean Star."
The Romance of Jenny Harlowe.

On the Fo'k'sle Head. Post 8vo, illustrated boards, 2s.
An Ocean Tragedy: A Novel. Three Vols., crown 8vo.

Sala.—Gaslight and Daylight.
By GEORGE AUGUSTUS SALA. Post 8vo, illustrated boards, 2s.

Sanson.—Seven Generations of Executioners: Memoirs of the Sanson Family (1688 to 1847). Edited by HENRY SANSON. Cr.8vo,cl.ex.3s.6d.

Saunders (John), Novels by:
Crown 8vo, cloth extra, 3s. 6d. each; post 8vo, illustrated boards, 2s. each.
Guy Waterman. | Lion in the Path.
The Two Dreamers.

Bound to the Wheel. Crown 8vo, cloth extra, 3s. 6d.

Saunders (Katharine), Novels by. Cr. 8vo, cloth extra, 3s. 6d. each; post 8vo, illustrated boards, 2s. each.
Margaret and Elizabeth.
The High Mills.
Heart Salvage. | Sebastian.

Joan Merryweather. Post 8vo, illustrated boards, 2s.
Gideon's Rock. Crown 8vo, cloth extra, 3s. 6d.

Science-Gossip for 1890: An Illustrated Medium of Interchange for Students and Lovers of Nature. Edited by Dr. J. E. TAYLOR, F.L.S.,&c. Devoted to Geology, Botany, Physiology, Chemistry, Zoology, Microscopy, Telescopy, Physiography, Photography,&c. Price 4d. Monthly; or 5s. per year, post-free. Vols. I. to XIX. may be had at 7s. 6d. each; and Vols. XX. to date, at 5s. each. Cases for Binding, 1s. 6d. each.

"Secret Out" Series, The:
Cr. 8vo, cl.ex., Illustrated, 4s. 6d. each.
The Secret Out: One Thousand Tricks with Cards, and other Recreations; with Entertaining Experiments in Drawing-room or "White Magic." By W.H.CREMER. 300Illusts.
The Art of Amusing: A Collection of Graceful Arts,Games,Tricks,Puzzles, and Charades By FRANK BELLEW. With 300 Illustrations.
Hanky-Panky: Very Easy Tricks, Very Difficult Tricks, White Magic, Sleight of Hand. Edited by W. H. CREMER. With 200 Illustrations.
Magician's Own Book: Performances with Cups and Balls, Eggs, Hats, Handkerchiefs, &c. All from actual Experience. Edited by W. H. CREMER. 200 Illustrations.

Seguin (L. G.), Works by:
The Country of the Passion Play, and the Highlands and Highlanders of Bavaria. With Map and 37 Illusts. and a NEW PREFACE for 1890. Crown 8vo, cloth extra, 3s. 6d.
Walks in Algiers and its Surroundings. With 2 Maps and 16 Illusts. Crown 8vo, cloth extra, 6s.

Senior.—By Stream and Sea.
By W. SENIOR. Post 8vo,cl.limp, 2s.6d.

Seven Sagas (The) of Prehistoric Man. By JAMES H. STODDART, Author of "The Village Life." Crown 8vo, cloth extra, 6s.

Shakespeare:
The First Folio Shakespeare.—MR. WILLIAM SHAKESPEARE'S Comedies, Histories, and Tragedies. Published according to the true Originall Copies. London, Printed by ISAAC IAGGARD and ED. BLOUNT. 1623.—A Reproduction of the extremely rare original, in reduced facsimile, by a photographic process—ensuring the strictest accuracy in every detail. Small 8vo, half-Roxburghe, 7s. 6d.
Shakespeare for Children: Tales from Shakespeare. By CHARLES and MARY LAMB. With numerous Illustrations, coloured and plain, by J. MOYR SMITH. Cr. 4to, cl. gilt, 6s.

Sharp.—Children of To-morrow: A Novel. By WILLIAM SHARP. Crown 8vo, cloth extra, 6s.

Shelley.—The Complete Works in Verse and Prose of Percy Bysshe Shelley. Edited, Prefaced and Annotated by R. HERNE SHEPHERD. Five Vols., cr. 8vo, cloth bds., 3s. 6d. each.

Poetical Works, in Three Vols.
Vol. I. An Introduction by the Editor; The Posthumous Fragments of Margaret Nicholson; Shelley's Correspondence with Stockdale; The Wandering Jew (the only complete version); Queen Mab, with the Notes; Alastor, and other Poems; Rosalind and Helen; Prometheus Unbound; Adonais, &c.
Vol. II. Laon and Cythna (as originally published, instead of the emasculated "Revolt of Islam"); The Cenci; Julian and Maddalo (from Shelley's manuscript); Swellfoot the Tyrant (from the copy in the Dyce Library at South Kensington); The Witch of Atlas; Epipsychidion; Hellas.
Vol. III. Posthumous Poems, published by Mrs. SHELLEY in 1824 and 1839; The Masque of Anarchy (from Shelley s manuscript); and other Pieces not brought together in the ordinary editions.

Prose Works, in Two Vols.
Vol. I. The Two Romances of Zastrozzi and St. Irvyne; the Dublin and Marlow Pamphlets; A Refutation of Deism; Letters to Leigh Hunt, and some Minor Writings and Fragments.
Vol. II. The Essays; Letters from Abroad; Translations and Fragments, Edited by Mrs. SHELLEY, and first published in 1840, with the addition of some Minor Pieces of great interest and rarity, including one recently dis overed by Professor DOWDEN. With a Bibliography of Shelley and an exhaustive Index of the Prose Works.

Sheridan(General).—Personal Memoirs of General P. H. Sheridan: The Romantic Career of a Great Soldier, told in his Own Words. With 22 Portraits and other Illustrations, 27 Maps, and numerous Facsimiles of Famous Letters. Two Vols. of 500 pages each, demy 8vo, cloth extra. 24s.

Sheridan (Richard Brinsley):
Sheridan's Complete Works, with Life and Anecdotes. Including his Dramatic Writings, printed from the Original Editions, his Works in Prose and Poetry, Translations, Speeches, Jokes, Puns, &c. With a Collection of Sheridaniana. Crown 8vo, cloth extra, gilt, with 10 full-page Tinted Illustrations, 7s. 6d.

Sheridan's Comedies: The Rivals, and The School for Scandal. Edited, with an Introduction and Notes to each Play, and a Biographical Sketch of Sheridan, by BRANDER MATTHEWS. With Decorative Vignettes and 10 full-page Illusts. Demy 8vo, half-parchment, 12s. 6d.

Sherard.—Rogues: A Novel. By R. H. SHERARD. Crown 8vo, picture cover, 1s.; cloth, 1s. 6d.

Sidney's (Sir Philip) Complete Poetical Works, including all those in "Arcadia." With Portrait, Memorial-Introduction, Notes, &c., by the Rev. A. B. GROSART, D.D. Three Vols., crown 8vo, cloth boards, 18s.

Signboards: Their History. With Anecdotes of Famous Taverns and Remarkable Characters. By JACOB LARWOOD and JOHN CAMDEN HOTTEN. With 100 Illustrations. Crown 8vo, cloth extra, 7s. 6d.

Sims (George R.), Works by:
Post 8vo, illustrated boards, 2s. each; cloth limp, 2s. 6d. each.
Rogues and Vagabonds.
The Ring o' Bells.
Mary Jane's Memoirs.
Mary Jane Married.
Tales of To-day.

Cr. 8vo, picture cover, 1s.ea.; cl., 1s.6d.ea.
The Dagonet Reciter and Reader Being Readings and Recitations in Prose and Verse, selected from his own Works by G. R. SIMS.
How the Poor Live; and Horrible London. In One Volume.

Sister Dora: A Biography. By MARGARET LONSDALE. Popular Edition, Revised, with additional Chapter, a New Dedication and Preface, and Four Illustrations. Sq. 8vo, picture cover, 4d.; cloth, 6d.

Sketchley.—A Match in the Dark. By ARTHUR SKETCHLEY. Post 8vo, illustrated boards, 2s.

Slang Dictionary, The: Etymological, Historical, and Anecdotal. Crown 8vo, cloth extra, 6s. 6d.

Smart.—Without Love or Licence: A Novel. By HAWLEY SMART. Three Vols., cr. 8vo.

Smith (J. Moyr), Works by:
The Prince of Argolis: A Story of the Old Greek Fairy Time. With 130 Illusts. Small 8vo, cloth extra. 3s. 6d.
Tales of Old Thule. With numerous Illustrations. Cr. 8vo, cloth gilt, 6s.
The Wooing of the Water Witch. With Illustrations. Small 8vo, 6s.

Society in London. By A FOREIGN RESIDENT. Crown 8vo, 1s.; cloth, 1s. 6d.

Society in Paris: The Upper Ten Thousand. A Series of Letters from Count PAUL VASILI to a Young French Diplomat. Trans. by R. L. DE BEAUFORT. Crown 8vo, cl. ex., 6s.

Society out of Town. By A FOREIGN RESIDENT, Author of "Society in London." Crown 8vo, cloth extra, 6s. [*Preparing.*

Somerset.—Songs of Adieu. By Lord HENRY SOMERSET. Small 4to, Japanese vellum, 6s.

Spalding.-Elizabethan Demonology: An Essay in Illustration of the Belief in the Existence of Devils, and the Powers possessed by Them. By T. A. SPALDING, LL.B. Cr. 8vo, cl. ex., 5s.

Speight (T. W.), Novels by:
The Mysteries of Heron Dyke. With a Frontispiece by M. ELLEN EDWARDS. Crown 8vo, cloth extra, 3s. 6d; post 8vo, illustrated bds., 2s.
Wife or No Wife? Post 8vo, cloth limp, 1s. 6d.
A Barren Title. Crown 8vo, cl., 1s. 6d.
The Golden Hoop. Post 8vo, illust. boards, 2s.
By Devious Ways; and A Barren Title. Post 8vo, illust. boards, 2s.
The Sandycroft Mystery. Crown 8vo, picture cover, 1s. [*Shortly.*

Spenser for Children. By M. H. TOWRY. With Illustrations by WALTER J. MORGAN. Crown 4to, cloth gilt, 6s.

Stageland: Curious Habits and Customs of its Inhabitants. By JEROME K. JEROME. With 64 Illustrations by J. BERNARD PARTRIDGE. Fourth Edition. Fcap. 4to, cl th extra, 3s. 6d.

Starry Heavens, The: A Poetical Birthday Book. Square 8vo, cloth extra, 2s 6d.

Staunton.—Laws and Practice of Chess. With an Analysis of the Openings. By HOWARD STAUNTON. Edited by ROBERT B. WORMALD. Small crown 8vo, cloth extra, 5s.

Stedman (E. C.), Works by:
Victorian Poets. Thirteenth Edition. Crown 8vo, cloth extra, 9s.
The Poets of America. Crown 8vo, cloth extra, 9s.

Sterndale.—The Afghan Knife: A Novel. By ROBERT ARMITAGE STERNDALE. Cr. 8vo, cloth extra, 3s 6d.; post 8vo, illustrated boards, 2s.

Stevenson (R.Louis),Works by: Post 8vo, cloth limp, 2s. 6d. each.
Travels with a Donkey in the Cevennes. Eighth Edition. With a Frontispiece by WALTER CRANE.
An Inland Voyage. Fourth Edition. With Frontispiece by WALTER CRANE.

STEVENSON (R. LOUIS), *continued—*
Cr. 8vo, buckram extra, gilt top, 6s. each.
Familiar Studies of Men and Books. Fifth Edition.
The Silverado Squatters. With Frontispiece. Third Edition.
The Merry Men. Second Edition.
Underwoods: Poems. Fourth Edit.
Memories & Portraits. Third Edit.
Virginibus Puerisque, and other Papers. Fifth Edition.

Cr. 8vo, buckram extra, gilt top, 6s. each; post 8vo, illust. boards, 2s. each.
New Arabian Nights. Eleventh Edit.
Prince Otto: Sixth Edition.

Stoddard.—Summer Cruising in the South Seas. By CHARLES WARREN STODDARD. Illustrated by WALLIS MACKAY. Crown 8vo, cloth extra, 3s. 6d.

Stories from Foreign Novelists. With Notices of their Lives and Writings. By HELEN and ALICE ZIMMERN. Frontispiece. Crown 8vo, cloth extra, 3s. 6d.; post 8vo, illust. bds., 2s.

Strange Manuscript (A) found in a Copper Cylinder. With 19 full-page Illustrations by GILBERT GAUL. Third Edition. Cr. 8vo, cl. extra, 5s.

Strange Secrets. Told by PERCY FITZGERALD, FLORENCE MARRYAT, JAMES GRANT, A. CONAN DOYLE, DUTTON COOK, and others. With 8 Illustrations by Sir JOHN GILBERT, WILLIAM SMALL, W. J. HENNESSY, &c. Crown 8vo, cloth extra, 6s.; post 8vo, illustrated boards, 2s.

Strutt's Sports and Pastimes of the People of England; including the Rural and Domestic Recreations, May Games, Mummeries, Shows, &c., from the Earliest Period to the Present Time. Edited by WM. HONE. With 140 Illustrations. Cr. 8vo, cl. extra, 7s. 6d.

Suburban Homes (The) of London: A Residential Guide to Favourite London Localities, their Society, Celebrities, and Associations. With Notes on their Rental, Rates, and House Accommodation. With Map of Suburban London. Cr.8vo.cl.ex.,7s 6d.

Swift (Dean) :—
Swift's Choice Works, in Prose and Verse. With Memoir, Portrait, and Facsimiles of the Maps in the Original Edition of "Gulliver's Travels." Crown 8vo, cloth extra, 7s. 6d.
A Monograph on Dean Swift. By J. CHURTON COLLINS. Crown 8vo, cloth extra, 8s. [*Shortly.*

Swinburne (Algernon C.), Works by:
Selections from the Poetical Works of A. C. Swinburne. Fcap. 8vo, 6s.
Atalanta in Calydon. Crown 8vo, 6s.
Chastelard. A Tragedy. Cr. 8vo, 7s.
Poems and Ballads. First Series. Cr. 8vo, 9s. Fcap. 8vo, same price.
Poems and Ballads. Second Series. Cr. 8vo, 9s. Fcap. 8vo, same price.
Poems and Ballads. Third Series. Crown 8vo, 7s.
Notes on Poems and Reviews. 8vo,1s.
Songs before Sunrise. Cr. 8vo, 10s.6d.
Bothwell: A Tragedy. Cr. 8vo,12s.6d.
George Chapman: An Essay. (See Vol. II. of Geo. Chapman's Works.) Crown 8vo, 6s.
Songs of Two Nations. Cr. 8vo, 6s.
Essays and Studies. Crown 8vo, 12s.
Erechtheus: A Tragedy. Cr. 8vo, 6s.
Songs of the Springtides. Cr. 8vo, 6s.
Studies in Song. Crown 8vo, 7s.
Mary Stuart: A Tragedy. Cr. 8vo, 8s.
Tristram of Lyonesse, and other Poems. Crown 8vo, 9s.
A Century of Roundels. Small 4to, 8s.
A Midsummer Holiday, and other Poems. Crown 8vo, 7s.
Marino Faliero: A Tragedy. Cr.8vo,6s.
A Study of Victor Hugo. Cr. 8vo, 6s.
Miscellanies. Crown 8vo, 12s.
Locrine: A Tragedy. Crown 8vo, 6s.
A Study of Ben Jonson. Cr. 8vo, 7s.

Symonds.—Wine, Women, and Song: Mediæval Latin Students' Songs. Now first translated into English Verse, with Essay by J. Addington Symonds. Small 8vo, parchment, 6s.

Syntax's (Dr.) Three Tours: In Search of the Picturesque, in Search of Consolation, and in Search of a Wife. With the whole of Rowlandson's droll Illustrations in Colours, and a Life of the Author by J. C. Hotten. Crown 8vo, cloth extra, 7s. 6d.

Taine's History of English Literature. Translated by Henry Van Laun. Four Vols., small 8vo, cloth boards, 30s.—Popular Edition, Two Vols., crown 8vo, cloth extra, 15s.

Taylor's (Bayard) Diversions of the Echo Club: Burlesques of Modern Writers. Post 8vo, cl. limp, 2s.

Taylor (Dr. J. E., F.L.S.), Works by. Crown 8vo, cloth ex., 7s. 6d. each.
The Sagacity and Morality of Plants: A Sketch of the Life and Conduct of the Vegetable Kingdom. Coloured Frontis. and 100 Illusts.
Our Common British Fossils, and Where to Find Them: A Handbook for Students. With 331 Illustrations.
The Playtime Naturalist. With 366 Illustrations. Crown 8vo, cl. ex., 5s.

Taylor's (Tom) Historical Dramas: "Clancarty," "Jeanne Darc," "'Twixt Axe and Crown," "The Fool's Revenge," "Arkwright's Wife," "Anne Boleyn," "Plot and Passion." One Vol., cr. 8vo, cloth extra, 7s. 6d.
** The Plays may also be had separately, at 1s. each.

Tennyson (Lord): A Biographical Sketch. By H. J. Jennings. With a Photograph-Portrait. Crown 8vo, cloth extra, 6s.

Thackerayana: Notes and Anecdotes. Illustrated by Hundreds of Sketches by William Makepeace Thackeray, depicting Humorous Incidents in his School-life, and Favourite Characters in the books of his every-day reading. With Coloured Frontispiece. Cr. 8vo, cl. extra, 7s. 6d.

Thames.—A New Pictorial History of the Thames. By A. S. Krausse. With 340 Illustrations. Post 8vo, picture cover, 1s.; cloth, 1s. 6d.

Thomas (Bertha), Novels by: Crown 8vo, cloth extra, 3s. 6d. each; post 8vo, illustrated boards, 2s. each.
Cressida. | Proud Maisie.
The Violin-Player.

Thomas (M.).—A Fight for Life: A Novel. By W. Moy Thomas. Post 8vo, illustrated boards, 2s.

Thomson's Seasons and Castle of Indolence. With Introduction by Allan Cunningham, and over 50 Illustrations on Steel and Wood. Crown 8vo, cloth extra, 7s. 6d.

Thornbury (Walter), Works by: Crown 8vo, cloth extra, 7s. 6d. each.
Haunted London. Edited by Edward Walford, M.A. With Illustrations by F. W. Fairholt, F.S.A.
The Life and Correspondence of J. M. W. Turner. Founded upon Letters and Papers furnished by his Friends and fellow Academicians. With numerous Illusts. in Colours.
Post 8vo, illustrated boards, 2s. each.
Old Stories Re-told.
Tales for the Marines.

Timbs (John), Works by: Crown 8vo, cloth extra, 7s. 6d. each.
The History of Clubs and Club Life in London. With Anecdotes of its Famous Coffee-houses, Hostelries, and Taverns. With many Illusts.
English Eccentrics and Eccentricities: Stories of Wealth and Fashion, Delusions, Impostures, and Fanatic Missions, Strange Sights and Sporting Scenes, Eccentric Artists, Theatrical Folk, Men of Letters, &c. With nearly 50 Illusts.

CHATTO & WINDUS, PICCADILLY. 25

Trollope (Anthony), Novels by:
Crown 8vo, cloth extra, 3s. 6d. each;
post 8vo, illustrated boards, 2s. each.
The Way We Live Now.
Kept in the Dark.
Frau Frohmann. | Marion Fay.
Mr. Scarborough's Family.
The Land-Leaguers.

Post 8vo, illustrated boards, 2s. each.
The Golden Lion of Granpere.
John Caldigate. | American Senator

Trollope (Frances E.), Novels by
Crown 8vo, cloth extra, 3s. 6d. each;
post 8vo, illustrated boards, 2s. each.
Like Ships upon the Sea.
Mabel's Progress. | Anne Furness.

**Trollope (T. A.).—Diamond Cut
Diamond,** and other Stories. By
T. ADOLPHUS TROLLOPE. Post 8vo,
illustrated boards, 2s.

Trowbridge.—Farnell's Folly:
A Novel. By J. T. TROWBRIDGE. Post
8vo, illustrated boards, 2s.

Tytler (C. C. Fraser-). — Mistress Judith: A Novel. By C. C.
FRASER-TYTLER. Cr. 8vo, cloth extra,
3s. 6d.; post 8vo, illust. boards, 2s.

Tytler (Sarah), Novels by:
Crown 8vo, cloth extra, 3s. 6d. each;
post 8vo, illustrated boards, 2s. each.
What She Came Through.
The Bride's Pass. | Noblesse Oblige.
Saint Mungo's City. | Lady Bell.
Beauty and the Beast.
Buried Diamonds.
The Blackhall Ghosts.

Post 8vo, illustrated boards, 2s. each.
Citoyenne Jacqueline.
Disappeared. | The Huguenot Family

**Van Laun.—History of French
Literature.** By H. VAN LAUN. Three
Vols., demy 8vo, cl. bds., 7s. 6d. each.

Villari.—A Double Bond. By L.
VILLARI. Fcap. 8vo, picture cover, 1s.

Walford (Edw., M.A.), Works by:
Walford's County Families of the
United Kingdom (1890). Containing
Notices of the Descent, Birth, Marriage, Education, &c., of more than
12,000 distinguished Heads of Families, their Heirs Apparent or Presumptive, the Offices they hold, their
Addresses, Clubs, &c. Twenty-ninth
Annual Ed. Royal 8vo, cl. gilt, 50s.
Walford's Shilling Peerage (1890).
Containing an Alphabetical List of
the House of Lords, Scotch and
Irish Peers, &c. 32mo, cloth, 1s.

WALFORD (EDWARD), *continued—*
Walford's Shilling Baronetage (1890).
Containing List of the Baronets of the
United Kingdom, Biographical Notices, Addresses, &c. 32mo, cloth, 1s.
Walford's Shilling Knightage (1890).
Containing an Alphabetical List of
the Knights of the United Kingdom,
short Biographical Notices, Dates of
Creation, Addresses, &c. 32mo, cl., 1s.
Walford's Shilling House of Commons (1890). Containing List of all
Members of Parliament, their Addresses, Clubs, &c. 32mo, cloth, 1s.
Walford's Complete Peerage, Baronetage, Knightage, and House of
Commons (1890). Royal 32mo,
cloth extra, gilt edges, 5s.
Walford's Windsor Peerage, Baronetage, and Knightage (1890).
Cr. 8vo, cloth extra, 12s. 6d.
William Pitt: A Biography. Post 8vo,
cloth extra, 5s.
Tales of our Great Families. A New
and Revised Edition. Crown 8vo,
cloth extra, 3s. 6d. [*Shortly*.
Haunted London. By WALTER THORNBURY. Edited by EDWARD WALFORD,
M.A. Illusts. by F. W. FAIRHOLT,
F.S.A. Cr. 8vo, cloth extra. 7s. 6d.

**Walton and Cotton's Complete
Angler;** or, The Contemplative Man's
Recreation. By IZAAK WALTON; and Instructions how to Angle for a Trout or
Grayling in a clear Stream, by CHARLES
COTTON. With Memoirs and Notes by
Sir HARRIS NICOLAS, and 61 Illusts.
Crown 8vo, cloth antique, 7s. 6d.

Walt Whitman, Poems by.
Selected and Edited, with an Introduction, by WILLIAM M. ROSSETTI. A
New Edition, with a Steel Plate Portrait. Crown 8vo, printed on handmade paper and bound in buckram, 6s.

Wanderer's Library, The:
Crown 8vo, cloth extra, 3s. 6d. each.
Wanderings in Patagonia; or, Life
among the Ostrich-Hunters. By
JULIUS BEERBOHM. Illustrated.
Camp Notes: Stories of Sport and
Adventure in Asia, Africa, and
America. By FREDERICK BOYLE.
Savage Life. By FREDERICK BOYLE.
Merrie England in the Olden Time.
By GEORGE DANIEL. With Illustrations by ROBT. CRUIKSHANK.
Circus Life and Circus Celebrities.
By THOMAS FROST.
The Lives of the Conjurers. By
THOMAS FROST.
The Old Showmen and the Old
London Fairs. By THOMAS FROST.
Low-Life Deeps. An Account of the
Strange Fish to be found there.· By
JAMES GREENWOOD.

BOOKS PUBLISHED BY

WANDERER'S LIBRARY, continued—
The Wilds of London. By JAMES GREENWOOD.
Tunis: The Land and the People. By the Chevalier de HESSE-WARTEGG. With 22 Illustrations.
The Life and Adventures of a Cheap Jack. Edited by CHARLES HINDLEY.
The World Behind the Scenes By PERCY FITZGERALD.
Tavern Anecdotes and Sayings. By CHARLES HINDLEY. With Illusts.
The Genial Showman: Life and Adventures of Artemus Ward. By E. P. HINGSTON. With a Frontispiece.
The Story of the London Parks. By JACOB LARWOOD. With Illusts.
London Characters. By HENRY MAYHEW. Illustrated.
Seven Generations of Executioners: Memoirs of the Sanson Family (1688 to 1847). Edited by HENRY SANSON.
Summer Cruising in the South Seas. By C. WARREN STODDARD. Illustrated by WALLIS MACKAY.

Warner.—A Roundabout Journey.
By CHARLES DUDLEY WARNER, Author of "My Summer in a Garden." Crown 8vo, cloth extra, 6s.

Warrants, &c. :—
Warrant to Execute Charles I. An exact Facsimile, with the Fifty-nine Signatures, and corresponding Seals. Carefully printed on paper to imitate the Original, 22 in. by 14 in. Price 2s.
Warrant to Execute Mary Queen of Scots. An exact Facsimile, including the Signature of Queen Elizabeth, and a Facsimile of the Great Seal. Beautifully printed on paper to imitate the Original MS. Price 2s.
Magna Charta. An exact Facsimile of the Original Document in the British Museum, printed on fine plate paper, nearly 3 feet long by 2 feet wide, with the Arms and Seals emblazoned in Gold and Colours. 5s.
The Roll of Battle Abbey; or, A List of the Principal Warriors who came over from Normandy with William the Conqueror, and Settled in this Country, A.D. 1066-7. With the principal Arms emblazoned in Gold and Colours. Price 5s.

Weather, How to Foretell the,
with the Pocket Spectroscope By F. W. CORY, M.R.C.S. Eng., F.R.Met. Soc., &c. With 10 Illustrations. Crown 8vo, 1s.; cloth, 1s. 6d.

Westropp.—Handbook of Pottery and Porcelain;
or, History of those Arts from the Earliest Period. By HODDER M. WESTROPP. With numerous Illustrations, and a List of Marks. Crown 8vo, cloth limp, 4s. 6d.

Whist. — How to Play Solo
Whist. With Specimen Hands in red and black, and Revised Code of Laws. By ABRAHAM S. WILKS and CHARLES F. PARDON. Crown 8vo, cloth extra, 3s. 6d.

Whistler's (Mr.) Ten o'Clock.
Crown 8vo, hand-made paper, 1s.

Williams (W. Mattieu, F.R.A.S.),
Works by:
Science in Short Chapters. Crown 8vo, cloth extra, 7s. 6d.
A Simple Treatise on Heat. With Illusts. Crown 8vo, cloth limp, 2s. 6d.
The Chemistry of Cookery. Crown 8vo, cloth extra, 6s.

Wilson (Dr. Andrew, F.R.S.E.),
Works by:
Chapters on Evolution: A Popular History of Darwinian and Allied Theories of Development. 3rd Ed. With 259 Illusts. Cr.8vo, cl. ex., 7s. 6d.
Leaves from a Naturalist's Notebook. Post 8vo, cloth limp, 2s. 6d.
Leisure-Time Studies, chiefly Biological. Third Edit. With numerous Illustrations. Cr. 8vo, cl. ex., 6s.
Studies in Life and Sense. With numerous Illusts. Cr. 8vo, cl. ex., 6s.
Common Accidents, and How to Treat them. By Dr. ANDREW WILSON and others. With numerous Illusts. Cr. 8vo, 1s.; cl. limp, 1s. 6d.

Winter (J. S.), Stories by:
Post 8vo, illustrated boards, 2s. each.
Cavalry Life. | Regimental Legends.

Wood.—Sabina: A Novel.
By Lady WOOD. Post 8vo, illust. bds., 2s.

Wood (H.F.), Detective Stories
by:
Crown 8vo, cloth extra, 6s. each; post 8vo, illustrated boards, 2s. each.
The Passenger from Scotland Yard.
The Englishman of the Rue Cain.

Woolley.—Rachel Armstrong;
or, Love and Theology. By CELIA PARKER WOOLLEY. Post 8vo, illustrated boards, 2s.; cloth, 2s. 6d.

Wright (Thomas), Works by:
Crown 8vo, cloth extra, 7s. 6d. each.
Caricature History of the Georges. (The House of Hanover.) With 400 Pictures, Caricatures, Squibs, Broadsides, Window Pictures, &c.
History of Caricature and of the Grotesque in Art, Literature, Sculpture, and Painting. Profusely Illustrated by F. W. FAIRHOLT, F.S.A.

Yates (Edmund), Novels by:
Post 8vo, illustrated boards, 2s. each.
Land at Last. | The Forlorn Hope.
Castaway.

THE PICCADILLY NOVELS.
Popular Stories by the Best Authors. LIBRARY EDITIONS, many Illustrated, crown 8vo, cloth extra, 3s. 6d. each.

BY GRANT ALLEN.
Philistia. | This Mortal Coil.
The Devil's Die | The Tents of Shem.

BY REV. S. BARING GOULD.
Red Spider. | Eve.

BY WALTER BESANT & J. RICE.
Ready-Money Mortiboy.
My Little Girl.
The Case of Mr. Lucraft.
This Son of Vulcan.
With Harp and Crown.
The Golden Butterfly.
By Celia's Arbour.
The Monks of Thelema.
'Twas in Trafalgar's Bay.
The Seamy Side.
The Ten Years' Tenant.
The Chaplain of the Fleet.

BY WALTER BESANT.
All Sorts and Conditions of Men.
The Captains' Room.
All in a Garden Fair.
Dorothy Forster. | Uncle Jack.
Children of Gibeon.
The World Went Very Well Then.
Herr Paulus.
For Faith and Freedom.

BY ROBERT BUCHANAN.
A Child of Nature.
God and the Man.
The Shadow of the Sword.
The Martyrdom of Madeline.
Love Me for Ever.
Annan Water. | The New Abelard
Matt. | Foxglove Manor.
The Master of the Mine.
The Heir of Linne.

BY HALL CAINE.
The Shadow of a Crime.
A Son of Hagar. | The Deemster.

BY MRS. H. LOVETT CAMERON.
Juliet's Guardian. | Deceivers Ever.

BY MORTIMER COLLINS.
Sweet Anne Page. | Transmigration.
From Midnight to Midnight.
MORTIMER & FRANCES COLLINS.
Blacksmith and Scholar.
The Village Comedy.
You Play me False.

BY WILKIE COLLINS.
Antonina. | Basil. | The Law and the
Hide and Seek. | Lady.
The Dead Secret | Haunted Hotel.
Queen of Hearts. | The Fallen Leaves
My Miscellanies. | Jezebel's Daughter
Woman in White. | The Black Robe.
The Moonstone. | Heart and Science
Man and Wife. | "I Say No."
Poor Miss Finch. | Little Novels.
Miss or Mrs.? | The Evil Genius.
New Magdalen. | The Legacy of
The Frozen Deep. | Cain.
The Two Destinies | A Rogue's Life.

BY DUTTON COOK.
Paul Foster's Daughter.

BY WILLIAM CYPLES.
Hearts of Gold.

BY ALPHONSE DAUDET.
The Evangelist; or, Port Salvation.

BY JAMES DE MILLE.
A Castle in Spain.

BY J. LEITH DERWENT.
Our Lady of Tears.
Circe's Lovers.

BY M. BETHAM-EDWARDS.
Felicia.

BY MRS. ANNIE EDWARDES.
Archie Lovell.

BY PERCY FITZGERALD.
Fatal Zero.

BY R. E. FRANCILLON.
Queen Cophetua. | A Real Queen.
One by One. | King or Knave?
Prefaced by Sir BARTLE FRERE.
Pandurang Hari.

BY EDWARD GARRETT.
The Capel Girls.

BY CHARLES GIBBON.
Robin Gray.
What will the World Say?
In Honour Bound.
Queen of the Meadow.
The Flower of the Forest.
A Heart's Problem.
The Braes of Yarrow.
The Golden Shaft.
Of High Degree.
Loving a Dream.

BY JULIAN HAWTHORNE.
Garth.
Ellice Quentin.
Sebastian Strome.
Dust.
Fortune's Fool.
Beatrix Randolph.
David Poindexter's Disappearance.
The Spectre of the Camera.

BY SIR A. HELPS.
Ivan de Biron.

BY ISAAC HENDERSON.
Agatha Page.

BY MRS. ALFRED HUNT.
Thornicroft's Model.
The Leaden Casket.
Self-Condemned.
That other Person.

BY JEAN INGELOW.
Fated to be Free.

BOOKS PUBLISHED BY

PICCADILLY NOVELS, continued—
BY R. ASHE KING.
A Drawn Game.
"The Wearing of the Green."

BY HENRY KINGSLEY.
Number Seventeen.

BY E. LYNN LINTON.
Patricia Kemball.
The Atonement of Leam Dundas.
The World Well Lost.
Under which Lord?
"My Love!"
Ione.
Paston Carew.

BY HENRY W. LUCY.
Gideon Fleyce.

BY JUSTIN McCARTHY.
The Waterdale Neighbours.
A Fair Saxon.
Dear Lady Disdain.
Miss Misanthrope.
Donna Quixote.
The Comet of a Season.
Maid of Athens.
Camiola.

BY AGNES MACDONELL.
Quaker Cousins.

BY FLORENCE MARRYAT.
Open! Sesame!

BY D. CHRISTIE MURRAY.
Life's Atonement. | Coals of Fire.
Joseph's Coat. | Val Strange.
A Model Father. | Hearts.
By the Gate of the Sea.
A Bit of Human Nature.
First Person Singular.
Cynic Fortune.
The Way of the World.

BY MRS. OLIPHANT.
Whiteladies.

BY OUIDA.
Held in Bondage. | Two Little Wooden
Strathmore. | Shoes.
Chandos. | In a Winter City.
Under Two Flags. | Ariadne.
Idalia. | Friendship.
Cecil Castle- | Moths.
  maine's Gage. | Pipistrello.
Tricotrin. | A Village Com-
Puck. | mune.
Folle Farine. | Bimbi.
A Dog of Flanders | Wanda.
Pascarel. | Frescoes.
Signa. | In Maremma
Princess Naprax- | Othmar.
  ine. | Guilderoy.

BY MARGARET A. PAUL.
Gentle and Simple.

PICCADILLY NOVELS, continued—
BY JAMES PAYN.
Lost Sir Massing- | A Grape from a
  berd. | Thorn.
Walter's Word. | Some Private
Less Black than | Views.
  We're Painted | The Canon's Ward.
By Proxy. | Glow-worm Tales.
High Spirits. | Talk of the Town.
Under One Roof. | In Peril and Pri-
A Confidential | vation.
  Agent. | Holiday Tasks.
From Exile. | The Mystery of
                   | Mirbridge.

BY E. C. PRICE.
Valentina. | The Foreigners.
Mrs. Lancaster's Rival.

BY CHARLES READE.
It is Never Too Late to Mend.
Hard Cash. | Peg Woffington.
Christie Johnstone.
Griffith Gaunt. | Foul Play.
The Double Marriage.
Love Me Little, Love Me Long.
The Cloister and the Hearth.
The Course of True Love
The Autobiography of a Thief.
Put Yourself in His Place.
A Terrible Temptation
The Wandering Heir. | A Simpleton.
A Woman-Hater. | Readiana.
Singleheart and Doubleface.
The Jilt.
Good Stories of Men and other Animals.

BY MRS. J. H. RIDDELL.
Her Mother's Darling.
Prince of Wales's Garden-Party.
Weird Stories.

BY F. W. ROBINSON.
Women are Strange.
The Hands of Justice.

BY JOHN SAUNDERS.
Bound to the Wheel.
Guy Waterman. | Two Dreamers.
The Lion in the Path.

BY KATHARINE SAUNDERS.
Margaret and Elizabeth.
Gideon's Rock. | Heart Salvage.
The High Mills. | Sebastian.

BY T. W. SPEIGHT.
The Mysteries of Heron Dyke.

BY R. A. STERNDALE.
The Afghan Knife.

BY BERTHA THOMAS.
Proud Maisie. | Cressida.
The Violin-Player.

BY ANTHONY TROLLOPE.
The Way we Live Now.
Frau Frohmann. | Marion Fay.
Kept in the Dark.
Mr. Scarborough's Family.
The Land-Leaguers.

CHATTO & WINDUS, PICCADILLY. 29

PICCADILLY NOVELS, continued—
BY FRANCES E. TROLLOPE.
Like Ships upon the Sea.
Anne Furness. | Mabel's Progress.
BY IVAN TURGENIEFF, &c.
Stories from Foreign Novelists.
BY C. C. FRASER-TYTLER.
Mistress Judith.

PICCADILLY NOVELS, continued—
BY SARAH TYTLER.
What She Came Through.
The Bride's Pass. | Saint Mungo's City.
Beauty and the Beast.
Noblesse Oblige.
Lady Bell. | Buried Diamonds.
The Blackhall Ghosts.

CHEAP EDITIONS OF POPULAR NOVELS.
Post 8vo, illustrated boards, 2s. each.

BY EDMOND ABOUT.
The Fellah.

BY HAMILTON AÏDÉ.
Carr of Carrlyon. | Confidences.

BY MRS. ALEXANDER.
Maid, Wife, or Widow?
Valerie's Fate.

BY GRANT ALLEN.
Strange Stories.
Philistia. | The Devil's Die.
Babylon. | This Mortal Coil.
In all Shades.
The Beckoning Hand.
For Maimie's Sake.

BY REV. S. BARING GOULD.
Red Spider. | Eve.

BY SHELSLEY BEAUCHAMP.
Grantley Grange.

BY WALTER BESANT & J. RICE.
Ready-Money Mortiboy.
With Harp and Crown.
This Son of Vulcan. | My Little Girl.
The Case of Mr. Lucraft.
The Golden Butterfly.
By Celia's Arbour.
The Monks of Thelema.
'Twas in Trafalgar's Bay.
The Seamy Side.
The Ten Years' Tenant.
The Chaplain of the Fleet.

BY WALTER BESANT.
All Sorts and Conditions of Men.
The Captains' Room.
All in a Garden Fair.
Dorothy Forster.
Uncle Jack.
Children of Gibeon.
The World Went Very Well Then.
Herr Paulus.

BY FREDERICK BOYLE.
Camp Notes. | Savage Life.
Chronicles of No-man's Land.

BY BRET HARTE.
An Heiress of Red Dog.
The Luck of Roaring Camp.
Californian Stories.
Gabriel Conroy. | Flip.
Maruja. | A Phyllis of the Sierras.

BY HAROLD BRYDGES.
Uncle Sam at Home.

BY ROBERT BUCHANAN.
The Shadow of | The Martyrdom
  the Sword. | of Madeline.
A Child of Nature. | Annan Water.
God and the Man. | The New Abelard.
Love Me for Ever. | Matt.
Foxglove Manor. | The Heir of Linne
The Master of the Mine.

BY HALL CAINE.
The Shadow of a Crime.
A Son of Hagar. | The Deemster.

BY COMMANDER CAMERON.
The Cruise of the "Black Prince."

BY MRS. LOVETT CAMERON.
Deceivers Ever. | Juliet's Guardian.

BY MACLAREN COBBAN.
The Cure of Souls.

BY C. ALLSTON COLLINS.
The Bar Sinister.

BY WILKIE COLLINS.
Antonina. | My Miscellanies.
Basil. | Woman in White.
Hide and Seek. | The Moonstone.
The Dead Secret. | Man and Wife
Queen of Hearts. | Poor Miss Finch.
Miss or Mrs.? | The Fallen Leaves.
New Magdalen. | Jezebel's Daughter
The Frozen Deep. | The Black Robe.
The Law and the | Heart and Science
  Lady. | "I Say No."
The Two Destinies | The Evil Genius.
Haunted Hotel. | Little Novels.
A Rogue's Life.

BY MORTIMER COLLINS.
Sweet Anne Page. | From Midnight to
Transmigration. | Midnight.
A Fight with Fortune.

MORTIMER & FRANCES COLLINS.
Sweet and Twenty. | Frances.
Blacksmith and Scholar.
The Village Comedy.
You Play me False.

BY M. J. COLQUHOUN.
Every Inch a Soldier.

BY MONCURE D. CONWAY.
Pine and Palm.

BY DUTTON COOK.
Leo. | Paul Foster's Daughter.

CHEAP POPULAR NOVELS, *continued*—
BY C. EGBERT CRADDOCK.
The Prophet of the Great Smoky Mountains.
BY WILLIAM CYPLES.
Hearts of Gold.
BY ALPHONSE DAUDET.
The Evangelist; or, Port Salvation.
BY JAMES DE MILLE.
A Castle in Spain
BY J. LEITH DERWENT.
Our Lady of Tears. | Circe's Lovers.
BY CHARLES DICKENS.
Sketches by Boz. | Oliver Twist.
Pickwick Papers. | Nicholas Nickleby
BY DICK DONOVAN.
The Man-Hunter.
Caught at Last!
BY MRS. ANNIE EDWARDES.
A Point of Honour. | Archie Lovell.
BY M. BETHAM-EDWARDS.
Felicia.
BY EDWARD EGGLESTON.
Roxy.
BY PERCY FITZGERALD.
Bella Donna. | Never Forgotten.
The Second Mrs. Tillotson.
Polly. | Fatal Zero.
Seventy-five Brooke Street.
The Lady of Brantome.
BY PERCY FITZGERALD, &c.
Strange Secrets.
BY ALBANY DE FONBLANQUE.
Filthy Lucre.
BY R. E. FRANCILLON.
Olympia. | Queen Cophetua.
One by One. | King or Knave.
A Real Queen. | Romances of Law.
BY HAROLD FREDERIC.
Seth's Brother's Wife.
BY HAIN FRISWELL.
One of Two.
BY EDWARD GARRETT.
The Capel Girls.
BY CHARLES GIBBON.
Robin Gray. | In Honour Bound
For Lack of Gold. | The Flower of the
What will the | Forest.
 World Say? | Braes of Yarrow.
In Love and War. | The Golden Shaft.
For the King. | Of High Degree.
In Pastures Green | Mead and Stream.
Queen of the Mea- | Loving a Dream.
 dow. | A Hard Knot.
A Heart's Problem | Heart's Delight.
The Dead Heart. | Blood-Money.
BY WILLIAM GILBERT.
Dr Austin's Guests. | James Duke.
The Wizard of the Mountain.
BY JOHN HABBERTON.
Brueton's Bayou. | Country Luck.
BY ANDREW HALLIDAY.
Every-Day Papers.

CHEAP POPULAR NOVELS, *continued*—
BY LADY DUFFUS HARDY.
Paul Wynter's Sacrifice.
BY THOMAS HARDY.
Under the Greenwood Tree.
BY J. BERWICK HARWOOD.
The Tenth Earl.
BY JULIAN HAWTHORNE.
Garth. | Sebastian Strome
Ellice Quentin. | Dust.
Fortune's Fool. | Beatrix Randolph;
Miss Cadogna. | Love—or a Name.
David Poindexter's Disappearance.
The Spectre of the Camera.
BY SIR ARTHUR HELPS.
Ivan de Biron.
BY MRS. CASHEL HOEY.
The Lover's Creed.
BY MRS. GEORGE HOOPER.
The House of Raby.
BY TIGHE HOPKINS.
'Twixt Love and Duty.
BY MRS. ALFRED HUNT.
Thornicroft's Model.
The Leaden Casket.
Self-Condemned. | That other Person
BY JEAN INGELOW.
Fated to be Free.
BY HARRIETT JAY.
The Dark Colleen.
The Queen of Connaught.
BY MARK KERSHAW.
Colonial Facts and Fictions.
BY R. ASHE KING.
A Drawn Game.
"The Wearing of the Green."
BY HENRY KINGSLEY.
Oakshott Castle
BY JOHN LEYS.
The Lindsays.
BY MARY LINSKILL.
In Exchange for a Soul.
BY E. LYNN LINTON.
Patricia Kemball.
The Atonement of Leam Dundas.
The World Well Lost.
Under which Lord? | Paston Carew.
With a Silken Thread.
The Rebel of the Family.
"My Love." | Ione.
BY HENRY W. LUCY.
Gideon Fleyce.
BY JUSTIN McCARTHY.
Dear Lady Disdain | Miss Misanthrope
The Waterdale | Donna Quixote.
 Neighbours. | The Comet of a
My Enemy's | Season.
 Daughter. | Maid of Athens.
A Fair Saxon. | Camiola.
Linley Rochford. |

CHEAP POPULAR NOVELS, continued—
BY AGNES MACDONELL.
Quaker Cousins.
BY KATHARINE S. MACQUOID.
The Evil Eye. | Lost Rose.
BY W. H. MALLOCK.
The New Republic.
BY FLORENCE MARRYAT.
Open! Sesame. | Fighting the Air.
A Harvest of Wild | Written in Fire.
Oats.
BY J. MASTERMAN.
Half-a-dozen Daughters.
BY BRANDER MATTHEWS.
A Secret of the Sea.
BY JEAN MIDDLEMASS.
Touch and Go. | Mr. Dorillion.
BY MRS. MOLESWORTH.
Hathercourt Rectory.
BY J. E. MUDDOCK.
Stories Weird and Wonderful.
BY D. CHRISTIE MURRAY.
A Life's Atonement | Hearts.
A Model Father. | Way of the World.
Joseph's Coat. | A Bit of Human
Coals of Fire. | Nature.
By the Gate of the | First Person Sin-
Val Strange [Sea. | gular.
Old Blazer's Hero. | Cynic Fortune.
One Traveller Returns.
BY HENRY MURRAY.
A Game of Bluff.
BY ALICE O'HANLON.
The Unforeseen. | Chance? or Fate?
BY GEORGES OHNET.
Doctor Rameau.
BY MRS. OLIPHANT.
Whiteladies. | The Primrose Path.
The Greatest Heiress in England.
BY MRS. ROBERT O'REILLY.
Phœbe's Fortunes.
BY OUIDA.
Held in Bondage. | Two Little Wooden
Strathmore. | Shoes.
Chandos. | Ariadne.
Under Two Flags. | Friendship.
Idalia. | Moths.
Cecil Castle- | Pipistrello.
maine's Gage. | A Village Com-
Tricotrin. | Puck. | mune.
Folle Farine. | Bimbi. | Wanda.
A Dog of Flanders. | Frescoes.
Pascarel. | In Maremma.
Signa. [ine. | Othmar.
Princess Naprax- | Ouida's Wisdom,
in a Winter City. | Wit, and Pathos.
BY MARGARET AGNES PAUL.
Gentle and Simple.
BY JAMES PAYN.
Lost Sir Massing- | A County Family.
berd. | At Her Mercy.
A Perfect Treasure | A Woman's Ven-
Bentinck's Tutor. | geance.
Murphy's Master. | Cecil's Tryst.

CHEAP POPULAR NOVELS, continued—
Clyffards of Clyffe | Mirk Abbey.
The Family Scape- | Less Black than
grace. | We're Painted
Foster Brothers. | By Proxy.
Found Dead. | Under One Roof.
Best of Husbands. | High Spirits.
Walter's Word. | Carlyon's Year.
Halves. | A Confidential
Fallen Fortunes. | Agent.
What He Cost Her | Some Private
Humorous Stories | Views.
Gwendoline's Har- | From Exile.
vest. | A Grape from a
£200 Reward. | Thorn.
Like Father, Like | For Cash Only.
Son. | Kit: A Memory.
Marine Residence. | The Canon's Ward
Married Beneath | Talk of the Town.
Him. | Holiday Tasks.
Not Wooed, but | Glow-worm Tales
Won. | The Mystery of Mirbridge.

BY C. L. PIRKIS.
Lady Lovelace.

BY EDGAR A. POE.
The Mystery of Marie Roget.

BY E. C. PRICE.
Valentina. | The Foreigners
Mrs. Lancaster's Rival.
Gerald.

BY CHARLES READE.
It is Never Too Late to Mend.
Hard Cash. | Peg Woffington.
Christie Johnstone.
Griffith Gaunt.
Put Yourself in His Place.
The Double Marriage.
Love Me Little, Love Me Long.
Foul Play.
The Cloister and the Hearth.
The Course of True Love.
Autobiography of a Thief.
A Terrible Temptation.
The Wandering Heir.
A Simpleton. | A Woman-Hater.
Readiana. | The Jilt.
Singleheart and Doubleface.
Good Stories of Men and other
Animals.

BY MRS. J. H. RIDDELL.
Her Mother's Darling.
Prince of Wales's Garden Party.
Weird Stories. | Fairy Water.
The Uninhabited House.
The Mystery in Palace Gardens.

BY F. W. ROBINSON
Women are Strange.
The Hands of Justice.

BY JAMES RUNCIMAN.
Skippers and Shellbacks.
Grace Balmaign's Sweetheart.
Schools and Scholars.

CHEAP POPULAR NOVELS, continued—

BY W. CLARK RUSSELL.
Round the Galley Fire.
On the Fo'k'sle Head.
In the Middle Watch.
A Voyage to the Cape.
A Book for the Hammock.
The Mystery of the "Ocean Star."
The Romance of Jenny Harlowe.

BY GEORGE AUGUSTUS SALA.
Gaslight and Daylight.

BY JOHN SAUNDERS.
Guy Waterman. | Two Dreamers.
The Lion in the Path.

BY KATHARINE SAUNDERS.
Joan Merryweather. | The High Mills.
Margaret and Elizabeth.
Heart Salvage. | Sebastian.

BY GEORGE R. SIMS.
Rogues and Vagabonds.
The Ring o' Bells. | Mary Jane Married.
Mary Jane's Memoirs.
Tales of To-day.

BY ARTHUR SKETCHLEY.
A Match in the Dark.

BY T. W. SPEIGHT.
The Mysteries of Heron Dyke.
The Golden Hoop. | By Devious Ways.

BY R. A. STERNDALE.
The Afghan Knife.

BY R. LOUIS STEVENSON.
New Arabian Nights. | Prince Otto.

BY BERTHA THOMAS.
Cressida. | Proud Maisie.
The Violin-Player.

BY W. MOY THOMAS.
A Fight for Life.

BY WALTER THORNBURY.
Tales for the Marines.
Old Stories Re-told.

BY T. ADOLPHUS TROLLOPE.
Diamond Cut Diamond.

BY ANTHONY TROLLOPE.
The Way We Live Now.
The American Senator.
Frau Frohmann. | Marion Fay.
Kept in the Dark.
Mr. Scarborough's Family.
The Land-Leaguers. | John Caldigate
The Golden Lion of Granpere.

By F. ELEANOR TROLLOPE.
Like Ships upon the Sea.
Anne Furness. | Mabel's Progress.

BY J. T. TROWBRIDGE.
Farnell's Folly.

BY IVAN TURGENIEFF, &c.
Stories from Foreign Novelists.

BY MARK TWAIN.
Tom Sawyer. | A Tramp Abroad.
The Stolen White Elephant.
A Pleasure Trip on the Continent
Huckleberry Finn. [of Europe.
Life on the Mississippi
The Prince and the Pauper.

CHEAP POPULAR NOVELS, continued—

BY C. C. FRASER-TYTLER.
Mistress Judith.

BY SARAH TYTLER.
What She Came Through.
The Bride's Pass. | Buried Diamonds.
Saint Mungo's City.
Beauty and the Beast.
Lady Bell. | Noblesse Oblige.
Citoyenne Jacqueline | Disappeared.
The Huguenot Family.
The Blackhall Ghosts.

BY J. S. WINTER.
Cavalry Life. | Regimental Legends.

BY H. F. WOOD.
The Passenger from Scotland Yard.
The Englishman of the Rue Cain.

BY LADY WOOD.
Sabina.

BY CELIA PARKER WOOLLEY.
Rachel Armstrong; or, Love&Theology.

BY EDMUND YATES.
The Forlorn Hope. | Land at Last.
Castaway.

ANONYMOUS.
Why Paul Ferroll Killed his Wife.

POPULAR SHILLING BOOKS.

Jeff Briggs's Love Story. By BRET HARTE.
The Twins of Table Mountain. By BRET HARTE.
A Day's Tour. By PERCY FITZGERALD.
Esther's Glove. By R. E. FRANCILLON.
The Professor's Wife. By L. GRAHAM.
Mrs. Gainsborough's Diamonds. By JULIAN HAWTHORNE.
Niagara Spray. By J. HOLLINGSHEAD.
A Romance of the Queen's Hounds. By CHARLES JAMES.
The Garden that Paid the Rent. By TOM JERROLD.
Cut by the Mess. By ARTHUR KEYSER.
Our Sensation Novel. Edited by JUSTIN H. MCCARTHY, M.P.
Dolly. By JUSTIN H. MCCARTHY, M.P.
Lily Lass. By JUSTIN H. MCCARTHY, M.P.
Was She Good or Bad? By W. MINTO.
That Girl in Black. By Mrs. MOLESWORTH.
Beyond the Gates. By E. S. PHELPS.
Old Maid's Paradise. By E. S. PHELPS.
Burglars in Paradise. By E. S. PHELPS.
Jack the Fisherman. By E. S. PHELPS.
Trooping with Crows. By C. L. PIRKIS
Bible Characters. By CHAS. READE.
Rogues. By R. H. SHERARD.
The Dagonet Reciter. By G. R. SIMS.
How the Poor Live. By G. R. SIMS.
The Sandycroft Mystery. By T. W. SPEIGHT.
A Double Bond. By LINDA VILLARI.

www.ingramcontent.com/pod-product-compliance
Lightning Source LLC
Chambersburg PA
CBHW022055230426
43672CB00008B/1181